Dissertations
in
American Economic History

This is a volume in the Arno Press collection

Dissertations
in
American Economic History

Advisory Editor
Stuart Bruchey

Research Associate
Eleanor Bruchey

*See last pages of this volume
for a complete list of titles.*

INVESTMENT BEHAVIOR
BY UNITED STATES RAILROADS,
1870-1914

James Reed Golden

ARNO PRESS
A New York Times Company
New York – 1975

First publication in book form, Arno Press, 1975

Copyright © 1975 by James Reed Golden

DISSERTATIONS IN AMERICAN ECONOMIC HISTORY
ISBN for complete set: 0-405-07252-X
See last pages of this volume for titles.

Manufactured in the United States of America

Publisher's Note: This thesis was reproduced
from the best available copy.

————◆————

Library of Congress Cataloging in Publication Data

Golden, James Reed.
    Investment behavior by United States railroads,
1870-1914.

    (Dissertations in American economic history)
    Originally presented as the author's thesis, Harvard,
1971.
    Bibliography: p.
    1. Railroads--United States--Finance--History.
2. Investments--United States--History. I. Title.
II. Series.
HE2236.G64 1975   385'.1   75-2582
ISBN 0-405-07202-3

"Investment Behavior by United States Railroads, 1870-1914"

A thesis presented

by

James Reed Golden

to

The Department of Economics

in partial fulfillment of the requirements

for the degree of

Doctor of Philosophy

in the subject of

Economics

Harvard University

Cambridge, Massachusetts

August, 1971

TABLE OF CONTENTS

iv

LIST OF TABLES

vii

viii

LIST OF FIGURES

CHAPTER I

INTRODUCTION

Purpose

The geneology of this study of investment in the railroad sector is long and illustrious, and it is possible that
the offspring is more distinguished from its forebears by
ambition than insight. The sector has been a source of
fruitful study of investment behavior because of its long
and well documented statistical history. The extension of
the analysis to periods earlier than 1914, however, has
raised considerable controversy over the validity of aggregate investment and capital series stretching back to 1870
and over the statistical studies of investment behavior
based on that data.

The objective of this study is to develop a consistent
statistical base for the analysis of investment by United
States railroads in the period from 1870 to 1914, to determine the extent to which mensurable market variables as defined by investment theory "explain" annual variations in
investment, and to combine the statistical results with
qualitative evidence in an analysis of changing investment
patterns. Particular emphasis is placed on the proper
measurement of the relevant variables, especially on the

1

impact of technical change on the measurement of capital capacity, and on tests to establish the validity of the statistical estimates. The results of the study are compared with former investigations of the sector and are used to confront the thesis that investment behavior in the sector varied in a predictable manner over its "life-cycle".

Background

The heterogeneous grouping of concepts that has come to be known as investment theory owes a considerable debt to early empirical tests based largely on railroad records. J. M. Clark's (1917) graphical analysis of railroad car orders provided the impetus to a broad spectrum of acceleration theories when he observed that the "demand for cars varies with the rate at which traffic is increasing or diminishing rather than with the absolute volume of the traffic."[1] Clark's accelerator theory was modified by a more comprehensive understanding of the relevant assumptions than later writers attributed to him. Studies by Kuznets (1935),[2] Tinbergen (1938),[3] Manne

---

[1]J. M. Clark, "Business Acceleration and the Law of Demand: A Technical Factor in Economic Cycles," Journal of Political Economy (March, 1917), pp. 217-235.

[2]Simon Kuznets, "Relation Between Capital Goods and Finished Products in the Business Cycle," in Economic Essays in Honour of Wesley Clair Mitchell (New York: 1935).

[3]Jan Tinbergen, Statistical Testing of Business Cycle Theories (Geneva: League of Nations, 1939).

(1945),[4] Klein (1951),[5] Leontief (1951)[6] and Koyck (1954)[7] drew heavily or exclusively on the railroad sector and provided a large part of the early empirical testing of investment theory.

A more recent off-shoot of the bifurcated analysis of investment over the business cycle proposed by Meyer and Kuh (1957),[8] Kuh (1963),[9] and Meyer and Glauber (1964)[10] has been an attempt to associate different patterns of investment behavior with different positions in an industry's "life-cycle". To develop this thesis Kmenta and Williamson

---

[4]Alan S. Manne, "Some Notes on the Acceleration Principle," Review of Economics and Statistics, Vol. 27 (May, 1945), pp. 93-99.

[5]Lawrence R. Klein, "Studies in Investment Behavior," in Conference on Business Cycles (New York: National Bureau of Economic Research, 1951), pp. 233-303.

[6]Wassily Leontief, "A Comment on Klein's Studies in Investment Behavior," in Conference on Business Cycles (New York: National Bureau of Economic Research, 1951), pp. 310-313.

[7]L. M. Koyck, Distributed Lags and Investment Analysis (Amsterdam: North Holland Pub. Co., 1954).

[8]John R. Meyer and Edwin Kuh, The Investment Decision (3rd ed; Cambridge: Harvard University Press, 1966).

[9]Edwin Kuh, Capital Stock Growth: A Micro-Econometric Approach (Amsterdam: North Holland Publishing Co., 1963).

[10]John R. Meyer and Robert R. Glauber, Investment Decisions, Economic Forecasting and Public Policy (Boston: Harvard University Press, 1964).

(1966)[11] drew upon the Ulmer (1960)[12] capital series for the railroad sector stretching back to 1870 and derived different investment behavioral patterns for periods of: "adolescence" - 1872 to 1895; "maturity" - 1896 to 1914; and "senility" - 1922 to 1941.[13] The models they developed for each period based on the stage of growth model appeared to work best in the period for which they were designed, were statistically significant in the usual senses, and explained a larger portion of the variance of investment than more general models produced by other investigators.

The validity of the Ulmer capital and investment series used by Kmenta and Williamson had been challenged by Fishlow (1966)[14] and was further attacked by Neal (1969).[15] With

---

[11] Jan Kmenta and Jeffrey G. Williamson, "Determinants of Investment Behavior: United States Railroads, 1872-1941," The Review of Economics and Statistics, Vol. 48 (May, 1966), pp. 172-181.

[12] Melville Ulmer, Capital in Transportation, Communications, and Public Utilities: Its Formation and Financing, National Bureau of Economic Research (Princeton: Princeton University Press, 1960).

[13] Jan Kmenta and Jeffrey Williamson, "Determinants of Investment Behavior," Op. Cit., p. 178.

[14] Albert Fishlow, "Productivity and Technological Change in the Railroad Sector, 1870-1910," in Studies in Income and Wealth XXX, Output, Employment, and Productivity in the United States After 1800 (New York: National Bureau of Economic Research, 1966), pp. 583-646.

[15] Larry Neal, "Investment Behavior by American Railroads, 1897-1914," Review of Economics and Statistics (May, 1969), pp. 126-135.

new series of capital and investment derived from company
reports Neal found that investment in the sector in the
period from 1897 to 1914 could best be explained by the impact of financial factors, rather than the accelerator model
proposed by Kmenta and Williamson and most other investigators for that period. Neal concluded:

> But this result does not reconstitute the life cycle
> hypothesis (in altered form) so much as it indicates
> the value of paying attention to the major features
> of an industry's economic history when attempting
> to explain its investment behavior. Such attention
> to economic history might also mitigate against
> facile acceptance of faulty data and the misleading
> results they may produce.[16]

Even with the best data, however, the use of aggregate
time series to distinguish among competing investment
theories is a hazardous business. The statistical problems are well known but bear restatement. First, the
theoretical basis of investment analysis is usually founded
on decisions made at the company level and least squares
estimation of the micro-coefficients using aggregate data
will in general produce biased estimates of those coefficients. Thiel showed that this bias can be eliminated if
weighted linear aggregates of the micro variables are used
to produce the macro variables, but the correct weights are
the micro-coefficients themselves![17] Second, there is the

---

[16]Ibid, p. 135.

[17]H. Thiel, Linear Aggregation of Economic Relations
(Amsterdam: North Holland Publishing Co., 1954), pp. 135-140.

problem of correctly identifying the single equation investment function. For example the level of earnings may play
a large role in determining investment, but the level of
investment may also influence the level of earnings. In
general one equation may produce reasonable predictions, but
many are needed to produce unbiased structural parameters.
Such identification problems are closely related to the
omission of relevant variables. The latter error may be
extremely important where the number of observations allow
the testing of a limited number of explanatory variables or
important explanatory variables cannot be quantified.
Third, where the number of observations is small the efficiency of least squares estimation is reduced.[18] This
error could be particularly significant in evaluating the
results obtained by Neal and Kmenta and Williamson, since
their largest sample size in any period is 24 and the
smallest is 17. Finally while autocorrelation of the error
terms in time series can be discovered and corrected, the
errors produced by multicollinearity in the explanatory
variables cannot, unless of course the multicollinearity is
perfect and the matrix is singular. Multicollinearity is
common in aggregate data and in such cases the allocation

---

[18]Leonid Hurwicz, "Least Squares Bias in Time Series,"
Statistical Inference in Dynamic Economic Models, Tjalling
C. Koopmans (ed), Cowles Commission Monograph No. 10 (New
York: Cowles Commission, 1950), pp. 365-384.

of explanatory power to competing explanatory variables is apt to be arbitrary. This problem is perhaps the most damaging where structural parameters are required to evaluate conflicting theories.

Many of these problems can be reduced by properly specifying the behavioral models and increasing the number of degrees of freedom for statistical testing. But where changes in the behavioral function are expected over time, simple extension of the aggregate series is an unacceptable solution. An alternate approach would be to employ the additional observations available in cross-section analysis. This is appealing because the unit of observation is the individual firm, the identification problem is reduced where firms follow a rigid price policy and revenues are determined from variations in demand, the number of observations can be increased dramatically, and multicollinearity is reduced. Size differences in the sample may produce an undesireable correlation of the error term variance with the dependent variable, but this heteroscedaticity effect can be detected and corrected by a transformation of variables or the elimination of large or small firms. If pooled cross-sections are used autocorrelation is also possible where error terms for particular firms are interdependent.

But unfortunately time series and cross-section coefficients are not directly comparable since different assumptions about the error term are required. For example, entrepreneurial ability may well be a constant for one firm over time but should vary from firm to firm at one point in time. Cross-section data also tend to reflect a more complete adjustment to long term equilibrium and coefficients have generally been larger in cross-section than time series studies. These factors led Kuh to conclude:

> One fairly obvious, but not trivial, negative conclusion is that cross-sections are likely to be a poor vehicle for testing hypotheses about investment or estimating parameters when dynamic disturbances are significant. However, with numerous cross-sections available, variations in the cross section estimates can be analyzed in order to provide substantive information about the time series specification.[19]

Scope

Kuh's observation on the use of cross-section data played a central role in the formulation of this study. The analysis of aggregate series for the sector over short time periods is beset with numerous statistical problems which make the interpretation of the results questionable. To increase the number of observations for statistical testing data from a sample of 19 firms, discussed in Appendix G, were used to augment revised aggregate data. Eighteen overlapping cross-sections containing observations on the firms over two or three year periods, based on the aggregate business cycle, were analyzed to isolate changes

---

[19]Edwin Kuh, Capital Stock Growth, Op. Cit., p. 328.

in investment policy over the cycle and to select the most
important variables for further analysis. The cross-section
results were used to assist in the specification of time
series equations for each sample company. The time series
results for different firms were compared for various components of investment over different periods and regional
groupings. The company time series and cross-section results were used in turn to clarify and modify the patterns
which emerged in the analysis of data for the sector as a
whole.

Method

The statistical results were used to clarify the qualitative evidence on investment behavior which is available
from a wealth of studies on the railroad sector in this
period. Chapter II provides an overview of the historical
setting of the sector from 1870 to 1914 by combining a synthesis of the qualitative material with a quantitative
record of price variations, output, employment, capital
efficiency, and total factor productivity. Chapter III presents a brief summary of investment and capital theory and
discusses previous studies of investment behavior in the
sector.

The following three chapters discuss the statistical
results. Chapter IV presents the results of tests with the
revised aggregate data and compares those results with

former studies. Chapter V outlines the cross-section analysis with emphasis on cyclical variations and variable significance. Chapter VI summarizes the time series results
for individual companies and analyzes regional, period, and
component patterns. Chapter VII provides a synthesis of the
aggregate, cross-section and time series results with the
qualitative record and presents a regional growth model
linked to variations in the regional distribution of companies, the availability of external financial funds, the
organizational structure of companies and changes in demand.
The implications of the results for sector life cycle
theories complete the analysis.

Most statistical derivations were restricted to the
Appendixes to simplify the exposition rather than minimize
their importance. Appendixes A, B and C derive annual sector output, employment, and price series respectively. Appendix D traces the derivation of the capital and investment series employing the estimates of changing capital
component efficiency in Appendix E. Appendix F presents
the aggregate regression results in detail. Appendix G
describes the process of selecting sample firms and discusses the characteristics of the sample. Finally, Appendix
H presents the detailed results of the company cross-section
and time series regression analysis.

CHAPTER II

OVERVIEW OF THE RAILROAD SECTOR: 1870-1914

Introduction

In 1876 Walt Whitman paid homage to the locomotive and its symbolic impact when he termed it: "Type of the modern emblem of motion and power - pulse of the continent."[1] Yet as he wrote over twenty percent of all railroad mileage in the United States was operated by receivers.[2] The wave of expansion which carried iron rail to the Pacific had crashed three years earlier in financial chaos. Even the exhilaration of the first transcontinental road had been tarnished in the presidential campaign of 1872 when the New York Sun exposed the extent of the Credit Mobilier construction scandal. In 1873 Mark Twain reflected the growing thrust of public sentiment when he criticized the excesses of railroad entrepreneurs in The Gilded Age:

> Duff Brown, the great railroad contractor, . . . a
> very pleasant man if you were not in his way, . . .

---

[1]Walt Whitman, "To a Locomotive in Winter," in Norman Foerster (ed), American Poetry and Prose (4th ed; Boston: Houghton Mifflin, 1957), p. 914.

[2]D. Philip Locklin, Economics of Transportation (5th ed rev; Homewood, Illinois: D. Irwin, Inc., 1960), p. 547.

managed to get out of Congress, in appropriations,
about weight for weight of gold for the stone fur-
nished.[3]

The visions of Whitman and Twain, both characteristi-
cally exaggerated, reflect the two dominant trends which
impacted on investment in the railroad sector from 1870 to
1914. The technological performance of the sector was impressive. The increase in total factor productivity, im-
perfectly reflected in substantial declines in real freight
and passenger rates, and the growth of output were unmatched
by any other sector of the economy. Yet the transformation
of the railroad sector was not accomplished without trauma.
Repeated cyclical over-expansion produced severe crises in
1873, 1884, 1893, and 1907 which threatened to tear assunder
what entrepreneurs had often too delicately joined together.

The period from 1870 to 1893 was characterized by
spurts of main track extension into new regions, partially
stimulated by high grain prices, followed by reductions in
grain prices, falling profit levels, and an evaporation of
finance capital. In the face of falling profits and increased fixed interest payments arising from the recent expansion, roads were forced to lower their rates and compete
for the available traffic. Restrictions to firm entry into
the sector were reduced by the opportunity to reorganize

---

[3]Mark Twain and Charles Werner, The Gilded Age, quoted
in American Poetry and Prose, Op. Cit., p. 947.

defunct lines with reduced capitalization and compete with established lines on favorable terms. While government control remained minimal, sharp competition for future monopoly positions served to eliminate effective cooperation between roads. Continuing expansion was insured by the lure of high future profits, but expansion also made the sector extremely susceptible to cyclical instability.

The pattern of reorganizations after the crisis in 1893 and the reduced importance of regional expansion altered this cyclical model. Banking interests with access to expanded bond markets gained increasing control of the sector and nurtured the trend toward consolidation of large systems. Government control became increasingly effective and by the end of the period played a significant role in the pattern of mergers and rate policy. The reduced importance of regional main track extension was reflected by the growing contribution of auxiliary track and rolling stock to total railroad capital.

Investment behavior in the sector was thus influenced by five central factors which form the major divisions of the remainder of this chapter: (1) the dramatic increase in total factor productivity, (2) the cyclical, regional and compositional structure of expenditures, (3) consolidation under the control of financial institutions, (4) the pattern of government control, (5) variations in the sources of investment finance.

Total Factor Productivity

When the last spike joining the Union Pacific and the Central Pacific was driven at Ogden, Utah, on May 10, 1869, the system of track east of the Alleghenies was generally completed, a skeletal system had been extended to the Mississippi, and the Santa Fe and Northern Pacific had begun construction of alternate routes to the Pacific. The standard 33 ton American (4-4-0) locomotive, praised by Whitman, hauled eleven ton freight cars over iron rail of varying gauges.[4] Rolling stock represented roughly three percent of total capital[5] and there were five miles of main line for every mile of auxiliary track.

Four decades later the railroad network was virtually complete. Mammouth 72 ton locomotives like the articulated Mallet (2-8-8-8-2) pulled eighteen ton freight cars, with triple the capacity of their smaller ancestors, over a standardized system of steel rail. Rolling stock accounted for more than twenty percent of total capital and there were only two miles of main track for every mile of auxiliary track.

Table E-2 traces the dramatic pace of the changing efficiency of track, locomotives, passenger cars and freight cars from 1870 to 1914. The capacity of track and locomotives,

---

[4]Table D4.

[5]Table F1.

measured by load capacity and tractive power respectively,
more than doubled, while freight car load capacity almost
tripled and passenger car volume increased by about fifty
percent. The substitution of steel for iron rail and the
steady increase in the size of rolling stock produced these
substantial changes with only marginal increases in operating costs. Since the process of innovation was continuous
and proceeded at a steady rate, dissemination of technical
advances was accomplished in the normal process of replacement rather than immediate substitution in Schumpeterian
investment waves. While the pace of technical change is
striking it is unlikely that it had any direct impact on the
observed cyclical pattern of investment.

Similarly the final standardization of track gauge and
integration of the railroad network proceeded gradually and
had a small impact on investment behavior. The Erie was
still laying third track to accomodate varying car gauges
as late as 1878 and the Southern roads did not make the final
shift to the standard 4' 8-1/2" gauge until 1886.[6] But integration of the system was virtually complete by 1870 with
the use of car hoists to accomodate gauge changes, and fast
freight lines which transferred cars over different roads
accounted for almost all through traffic. Thus it is

---

[6]George Rogers Taylor and Irene D. Neu, The American
Railroad Network, 1861-1890 (Cambridge: Harvard University
Press, 1956), pp. 79-81.

difficult to detect any significant break-throughs in technical innovation or integration of the railroad network which might have triggered significant changes in investment behavior.

The rate of technical change in individual capital components was matched by sharp increases in total factor productivity and output over the period from 1870 to 1914. Indeed no other sector grew as rapidly or recorded such large productivity gains. Table 2.1 portrays the relevant decadal data. Total output, derived in Table A3, increased by slightly over seven percent per year, which as Fishlow notes was largely based on geographic extension.

> From 1859 to 1910 geographic extension bears the largest share of the explanation of output growth. Mileage in use increased just about twice as rapidly as traffic density, and if we credit the lengthening of average haul to the influence of extension as well, the role of geographic widening in output growth is 2.2 times that of intensified demand.[7]

The composition of output remained quite constant in the face of rapid expansion with passenger revenue equal to about one-third of freight revenue in every period.[8]

The increase in output was matched by parallel increases in fuel consumption but employment and capital grew less

-----

[7]Albert Fishlow, "Productivity and Technological Change in the Railroad Sector," Op. Cit., p. 628.

[8]Bureau of Census, Historical Statistics of the United States, Colonial Times to 1957 (Washington: GPO, 1960), Series Q 23, Q 27, Q 71, and Q 84, pp. 428, 430, 431.

Table 2.1

SUMMARY OF RAILROAD OUTPUT, INPUT, AND PRODUCTIVITY, 1910=100

Year	1	2	3	4	5	6	7	8
1870	5.9	14.2	11.1	5.4	12.1	48.8	7.7	4.8
1880	13.3	24.7	18.6	11.7	21.1	63.0	6.5	4.7
1890	31.5	44.1	43.2	28.7	42.2	74.6	6.1	6.1
1900	54.6	59.9	60.4	45.9	58.7	93.0	5.0	6.3
1910	100.0	100.0	100.0	100.0	100.0	100.0	4.4	6.3

Column   Description

Year   Figures are for June 30 of the year listed. The
          capital stock in column 3 for 1870 is for 1871.

1   Output index derived in Table A3.

2   Railroad employment index based on Table B2.

3   Gross track and equipment capital stock index
          based on the series derived in Appendix D and
          listed in Table F1.

4   Fuel input index derived by Albert Fishlow,
          "Productivity and Technological Change in the
          Railroad Sector," Op. Cit., p. 626.

5   Total inputs series derived as a weighted sum of
          persons employed, capital and fuel, using
          weights of .52, .38, and .10 for columns 2
          through 5 respectively. The weights are the
          proportional shares of each factor in 1910
          output determined by the ICC and cited by
          Albert Fishlow, Ibid.

6   Total factor productivity defined as output in col-
          umn 1 divided by total inputs in column 5.

7   The gross capital-output ratio based on data in
          Table F1.

8   The gross capital-labor ratio computed as gross
          track and equipment capital from Table F1 divid-
          ed by the number employed taken from Table B2.

rapidly leading to the impressive increase in total factor productivity. Table 2.1 records the relevant decadal data for 1870 to 1910. The gross capital estimates in 1910 dollars are derived in Appendix D by adjusting component purchases and retirements for changing capital efficiency over time, but no productivity correction is applied to the employment estimates derived in Appendix B. The capital-labor ratio in these terms increased slightly over the period, but any significant correction for increasing labor efficiency would reverse this trend. While total factor productivity more than doubled over the period, the capital-output ratio fell from 7.7 in 1870 to 4.4 in 1910. Fishlow's capital and output figures for 1870 and 1910 produce corresponding ratios of 10.3 and 3.7.[9] The discrepancy arises because Fishlow's capital series is based on 1910 reproduction cost adjusted for depreciation in value, and my capital series is based on 1910 efficiency units. Ulmer's data produce an extraordinary decline in the capital-output ratio from 16.0 in 1880 to 4.4 in 1910, principally because of his high capital estimate for 1880.[10] Nevertheless it is clear that output per worker expanded significantly in the face of a declining capital-output ratio.

---

[9]Albert Fishlow, "Productivity and Technological Change in the Railroad Sector," Op. Cit., p. 631.

[10]Melville Ulmer, Capital in Transportation, Op. Cit., p. 70. See Appendix D for an analysis of Ulmer's capital estimates.

The first step in isolating the sources of the large increase in total factor productivity is an adjustment for the changing efficiency of labor. Until this correction is applied it is difficult to speculate on the relative importance of the increasing utilization of capital capacity, economies of scale in the sector, or improvements in the use of rolling stock. Indeed a more fruitful approach may be to examine variations in regional aggregates or even individual company reports to isolate the impact of these factors.

The advance in total factor productivity was reflected by a corresponding reduction in railroad freight and passenger rates from 1870 to 1910 as reflected in Table 2.2.

Table 2.2

REVENUE PER PASSENGER- AND TON-MILE (CENTS)

Year	Passenger[a]	Freight[a]	Passenger[b]	Freight[b]
	(Current $)		(1910 $)	
1870	2.80	2.18	3.42	2.66
1880	2.51	1.29	3.47	1.79
1890	2.17	.94	3.02	1.32
1900	2.00	.73	2.43	.89
1910	1.94	.75	1.94	.75

[a]Figures for 1870 to 1890 are from Table A2. Figures for 1900 and 1910 are from ICC, Statistics of Railways in the United States, as cited by Bureau of Census, Historical Statistics, Op. Cit., Series Q 72 and Q 86, pp. 430-431.

[b]Corresponding current price series divided by the capital price index in Table C3.

In terms of the relative cost of railroad capital goods the
rate per ton-mile in 1910 was less than one-third the rate
in 1870, and the passenger rate was one-half its 1870 level.
The permanence of much railroad capital made roads particularly vulnerable to rate competition when pools and other
market agreements failed, and the ease of entry at low
capitalization by reorganizing defunct lines provided steady
pressure on the rate structure.

Investment Patterns

Three dominant patterns may be noted in the changing
structure of investment from 1870 to 1914: (1) cyclical
periods of rapid expansion followed by financial crises and
reorganization, (2) a shifting regional concentration of
main track extension, (3) an increasing proportionate investment in auxiliary track and rolling stock. Figure D2 plots
the annual variations in gross railroad investment and suggests long cycle divisions from 1875 to 1895 and from 1896
to 1914. The year 1895 thus provides a convenient dividing
line for the analysis of investment trends.

By 1870 the railroad system east of the Alleghenies was
virtually complete and such venerable roads as the Baltimore
and Ohio and the Pennsylvania had already registered a clear
defeat of canal competitors and survived four decades of
tumultuous expansion. The feverish extension into the Upper
Mississippi Valley from 1867 to 1873 saw railroad mileage

operated increase from 39,050 to 70,268,[11] an enormous investment stimulated by high grain prices and booming land
values. The crisis in 1873, triggered by the reversal of
wheat prices and the failure of Jay Cooke and his Northern
Pacific, halted that expansion. Total railroad mileage in
the hands of receivers doubled from 1873 to 1874 and more
than tripled from 1874 to 1875.[12] Recovery from the depression proceeded slowly and railroad construction came to
a virtual halt until the European crop failure of 1879 and
a renewed boom in grain areas.

Periods of reduced demand produced the sharpest competition for traffic, as roads encumbered by new debts from
previous expansion struggled to cover interest payments
against new insolvent rivals. From 1875 to 1879 the Middle
Atlantic trunk lines were unable to maintain pool agreements
and rate wars periodically erupted among the New York Central, the Pennsylvania, the Baltimore and Ohio and the Erie.
The rate differentials apparently had a small impact on the
relative growth of the coastal cities since ocean freight
rates adjusted to the disparities and harbor facilities

---

[11]Bureau of Census, Historical Statistics, Op. Cit.,
Series Q 15, p. 427.

[12]D. Philip Locklin, Economics of Transportation, Op.
Cit., p. 547.

played a larger role in determining the allocation of
trade.[13] It soon became obvious that the fixed interest
position of a railroad largely determined its vulnerability
to rate competition, and that the reorganization of defunct
lines provided an ideal base for future competition. The
infamous "Nickel Plate" road was constructed parallel to the
Lake Shore and sold at a substantial profit to the harassed
New York Central in 1881, and in 1883 the West Shore provided a new threat to the Central from the opposite bank of
the Hudson. This pattern was not unique to Eastern roads.
In 1879 Jay Gould, a master at the art of financial manipulation, forced the merger of the defunct Denver and Pacific
with the Union Pacific at a large profit. Indeed one of the
recurring criticisms of the construction wave from 1879 to
1883 was the extent of such schemes devoted to construction
profits or blackmail rather than demand projections.[14]

> New roads were built, or sets of detached ones were
> connected, so as to afford additional parallels to
> the existing trunk lines, with no other object than
> to compel the latter to support them by dividing
> with them a portion of their traffic, or to accept
> the alternative of a reckless cutting down of rates.[15]

---

[13]Arthur T. Hadley, Railroad Transportation, Its History
and Laws (New York: G. P. Putnam's Sons, 1899), pp. 74, 98.

[14]Ibid, pp. 80-2. William Z. Ripley, Railroads, Finance
and Organization (New York: Longmans, Green and Co., 1915),
p. 22.

[15]Matthew Josephson, The Robber Barrons (New York:
Harcourt, Brace and Co., 1934), p. 189.

Hadley estimated that of the 29,000 miles of road built from 1880 to 1882 only one-third was justified by current demand, one-third had promise of future profits, and fully one-third was unnecessary extension for construction or blackmail profits.[16] A reversal of grain prices after 1882 ended the expansion and triggered numerous railroad failures. Villard's Northern Pacific managed to complete its final leg to the Pacific before declaring bankruptcy in 1884. In that year total mileage in receivership quadrupled and by 1885 it had doubled again. The ensuing construction lull lasted until roughly 1887 and was attributed by Henry Poor to the large number of speculative lines developed after 1878.[17]

Recovery from the crisis of 1884 was followed by three clear trends: (1) completion and expansion of transcontinental systems with buffers of branch lines between competitors, (2) a renewal of expansion of main track in the South and West, (3) an increasing emphasis on rolling stock and auxiliary track, particularly on the Eastern roads. Main track mileage in Poor's Northwest, Southwest and Pacific regions doubled between 1880 and 1890, matching the rate of expansion in the South Atlantic and Gulf and Mississippi

---

[16]Arthur T. Hadley, Railroad Transportation, Op. Cit., p. 38.

[17]Henry Poor, Manual of the Railroads, 1900, p. xliv.

Valley regions.[18] By 1900 main track extension in the East
and the Old Northwest was virtually complete, but extension
continued in the South and West. Between 1900 and 1920
main track mileage increased by only eight percent in New
England, the Middle Atlantic, and the Old Northwest, compared to 39 percent in the South, and 41 percent in the
Pacific, Southwest and Northwest regions using Stover's
classifications.[19]

The pattern of intensive investment on the Eastern
roads and extensive investment on Southern and Western roads
is reflected in the ratio of main to total track mileage,
since total track includes parallel lines as well as sidings
and yard track. ICC figures for 1900 indicate ratios of .61
and .60 for the Northeast and Middle Atlantic, and much
higher ratios of .83, .78, and .84 for the South, Northwest,
and Southwest respectively.[20] The Middle Atlantic which
contained 29 percent of total United States mileage in 1900
accounted for fully 48 percent of all revenue cars in service.[21] These regional differences may of course be linked
to different population densities and demand patterns, but

---

[18]Henry Poor, Manual of the Railroads, 1891, p. xviii.

[19]John F. Stover, American Railroads (Chicago: University of Chicago Press, 1961), pp. 223-4.

[20]ICC, Statistics of Railways in the United States for
1900, (Washington: GPO, 1901), p. 16.

[21]Ibid, p. 24.

it is clear that regional variations had a strong impact on
the explanation of aggregate investment behavior.

This pattern of regional expansion was interrupted by
the crisis of 1893 which was largely induced by failures in
the banking sector resulting from speculation on the future
of the gold standard. The crisis highlighted a fundamental
weakness in the railroad sector. Speculative expansion increased fixed interest obligations without providing sufficient current increases in net revenue to meet those obligations when confronted with cyclical reductions in demand.
Between 1894 and 1895 mileage in receivership quadrupled
including the huge Northern Pacific, Union Pacific, and
Santa Fe systems as well as the venerable Baltimore and Ohio.
The reorganization of the sector after 1895, largely controlled by banking interests, led to a significant consolidation of roads into major systems. The process of that
consolidation had a major impact on subsequent investment
patterns and is discussed in detail below.

The recovery and expansion after 1898 differed significantly from earlier construction waves. Henry Poor, who had
blamed earlier crises on the absorbing passion of the public,
noted that new lines were being built for earnings in response to current demand conditions.[22] Despite an increased
emphasis on debt financing the dividend record of the sector,

---

[22]Henry Poor, Manual of the Railroads, 1900, p. xliv.

reflected in Table 2.3, improved significantly. The consolidation of large systems limited the intense competition
which had plagued the sector prior to 1893, and the subsequent expansion was only briefly interrupted by the "rich

Table 2.3

PER CENT OF RAILROAD STOCK PAYING DIVIDENDS
(Selected Years 1876-1914)

Year	Per Cent[a]
1876	42
1884	44
1888	40
1893	40
1897	30
1907	67
1914	65

[a]For 1876 to 1888 figures are from Henry Poor, Manual
of the Railroads, as cited by Bureau of Census, Historical
Statistics, Op. Cit., Series Q 35 and Q 37, p. 428. For
1893 to 1914 data are from ICC, Statistics of the Railways,
as cited by Historical Statistics, Series Q 102, Q 98, and
Q 99, p. 433. Stock figures include common and preferred
stock.

man's panic" of 1907. The failure of several speculative
New York banks triggered the crisis which served to high-
light the problems of an inelastic currency system but had
a limited impact on the railroad sector as a whole. Mileage
in receivership initially doubled, but it quickly dropped
back to the 1906 level.

Even this cursory glance at the patterns of investment in the railroad sector from 1870 to 1914 is revealing. The cyclical response of investment to favorable profit conditions prior to 1895 tended to exceed the requirements of current demand, and subsequent competition for traffic forced a high percentage of roads into receivership. This pattern of cyclical over-expansion and excessive charges to construction expenses is reflected in the low percentage of stock paying dividends as shown in Table 2.3. Main track extension in the Northeast, Middle Atlantic and Old Northwest was largely completed by 1895, but extension in the South and West remained significant through 1914. Finally there was a marked increase in the proportionate investment in auxiliary track and rolling stock over the period centered primarily in the Northeast and Middle Atlantic regions.

Consolidation After 1895

The pattern of consolidation following the severe crisis of 1893 was largely based on the increasing prosperity after 1898 which allowed banking interests to float the large security issues required for reorganization. The banks argued that consolidation was the only solution to the problems of high interest payments and sharp competition which had characterized the sector prior to 1893, and sought to retain control of companies after reorganization and arrange for cooperation among their roads. As Nelson

concludes in <u>Merger Movements in American Industry 1895-1956</u>,
the principal explanation for the merger wave from 1898 to
1902 was the emergence of new strong capital markets and the
existence of institutions which enabled the organizers of
mergers to use those markets.[23]

The pattern of consolidation was similar whether the
reorganization was directed by Morgan through the First
National Bank, Rockefeller through the National City Bank,
or Harriman through Kuhn, Loeb and Company.

> Foreclosure was in each case followed by purchase
> of the property in behalf of former stockholders,
> who, as a condition to their participation in the
> new company, were assessed pro rata to raise the
> needed cash resources, the bondholders submitting
> to lower interest rates, usually receiving stock
> in the new corporation as a solace.[24]

Capitalization had no relation to property value. Debt was
issued up to the point where estimated earnings would cover
fixed charges and new stock was issued to satisfy all
equities.

> Since so many contingent and fixed annual obliga-
> tions were given precedence over common stock, its
> prospect of ever receiving a dividend was very re-
> mote. Consequently its market value stayed very
> low. This meant that if a company needed capital
> it must issue new bonds and within twenty years

---

[23]Ralph L. Nelson, <u>Merger Movements in American Industry
1895-1956</u> (Princeton: Princeton University Press, 1959),
pp. 1-59.

[24]E. G. Campbell, <u>The Reorganization of the American
Railroad System, 1893-1900</u> (New York: Columbia University
Press, 1938), p. 145.

after the turn of the century these circumstances
had led to a disproportionate increase in fixed
charges.[25]

Between July 1, 1899, and November 1, 1900, one-eighth
of all railroad mileage was brought under the control of
other lines, and by 1906 seven groups controlled over two-
thirds of all railroad mileage accounting for roughly 85
percent of gross railroad earnings.[26] Although the isolated
Rock Island system soon collapsed and the Gould system was
weakened by the failure of the Missouri Pacific in 1911, the
basic organization of the sector remained unchanged through
1914. The impact of this wave of consolidation on investment behavior was significant. Financiers maintained an
interest in the roads after reorganization and developed
communities of interest which extended beyond system limits.
Reduced competition raised the prospect of higher profits.
Finally the pattern of reorganization made further investment dependent on increased debt or the use of retained
earnings.

Role of Government

Government control of the railroad sector remained insignificant until the end of the period from 1870 to 1914.
First state governments and then the federal government

---

[25]Ibid, p. 322.

[26]Harold U. Faulkner, The Decline of Laissez Faire,
1897-1917 (New York: Harper and Row, 1968), pp. 191, 197.

sought to regulate the sector, but state control was limited
by the interstate character of railroad traffic and federal
control was reduced by repeated court decisions favoring
the carriers. The Hepburn Act of 1906 and the Mann-Elkins
Act of 1910 provided for the first significant control of
railroad rate policy.

In 1886 the Supreme Court reversed its earlier positions and ruled that states could not control commerce which
extended beyond their limits, and in 1889 it held that the
courts had the ultimate power to determine the reasonable-
ness of rates.[27] Since roughly 1869 the Granger movement,
centered in the Upper Mississippi Valley, had sought to control railroads through their state legislatures by revising
state constitutions and carefully wording railroad charters.
State railroad commissions were created to supervise the
sector although some, like the Massachusetts commission, had
only advisory powers. The Supreme Court decision of 1886
dictated that control must originate with the federal government.

The Interstate Commerce Act of 1887 was designed to
insure that rates were "reasonable" and to eliminate dis-
crimination among persons, localities, and distances. Kolko
has argued that railroads actively sought federal control of

---

[27]Harold U. Faulkner, American Economic History (8th
rev ed; New York: Harper and Row, 1966), p. 489.

rates to end costly competition since pool agreements had proven ineffective.

> In formulating a program designed to cope with the unpredictable control by the various states, and to protect themselves from their competitors or large shippers demanding expensive rebates, most railroad men approached the issue of regulation with purely opportunistic motives.[28]

If railroad men supported the concept of rate control in concept it is clear that many opposed it in practice. The Interstate Commerce Commission was given no binding authority to set rates and between 1887 and 1905 fifteen of the sixteen rate cases which reached the Supreme Court were decided for the carriers. The average period for rate litigation was roughly four years. The Supreme Court did hold in the Trans-Missouri Freight Association case of 1897 that pools were illegal and that railroads were subject to the Sherman Anti-Trust Act of 1890, but in the same year it declared that Congress had no authority to set rates but could only determine what rates were unfair.[29]

The Hepburn Act of 1906 gave the Interstate Commerce Commission the power to establish rates and to order compliance by the carriers, and directed the Commission to establish and enforce uniform accounting procedures. This act

---

[28]Gabriel Kolko, Railroads and Regulation 1877-1916 (Princeton: Princeton University Press, 1965), p. 4.

[29]Harold U. Faulkner, American Economic History, Op. Cit., pp. 490-1, 493.

transformed the Commission from an ineffective advisory body
into a strong regulatory agency. The Mann-Elkins Act of
1910 established a special Commerce Court to rule on railroad cases and gave the Commission the power to suspend new
rates for up to ten months pending investigation.

Government control of the railroad sector was thus more
limited than the record of state and federal legislation
might suggest. The merger movement was closely monitored
after 1897 under anti-trust laws, but rate control did not
become effective until 1906. The Interstate Commerce Commission served several useful functions in gathering statistics and publicizing rates, but had little impact on investment behavior in the sector as a whole until late in the
period.

Sources of Investment Finance

Several trends may be observed in the changing sources
of finance for railroad investment. First, there was a significant increase in the per cent of finance from retained
earnings after 1895. Second, there was a major change in
the role of financial intermediaries capable of tapping expanded capital markets after the recovery from the crisis of
1893. Finally, there was a steady increase in the ratio of
debt to total external finance.

Ulmer's data on the sources of investment funds probably overstate the extent of the shift from external to

internal finance after 1895.[30] The Hepburn Act of 1906
initiated a new depreciation accounting system and established depreciation reserves from which replacement expenditures could be made, while the old railroad system had been
to charge replacements to current expenditures. But under
the revised system charges to the depreciation reserve had
no relation to actual replacement outlays. Neal demonstrated
that replacement expenditures from 1908 to 1911 were much
lower than actual renewal charges.[31] Ulmer's data do not
include replacement expenditures prior to 1907 and assume
that such expenditures after 1907 equalled payments into the
depreciation reserve. Hence retained earnings account for
more than the 2.4% of total investment funds in 1880 to
1890 and 9.5% in 1893 to 1907 which he computed and less
than his 42.9% figure for 1907 to 1916.[32]

Applying an estimate of replacement expenditures from
the retirement model in Appendix D to Ulmer's figures for
the two earlier periods, and adjusting his depreciation reserve estimate for the latter period by the average ratio
of replacement expenditures to reserve charges observed by

---

[30]Melville Ulmer, Capital in Transportation, Op. Cit.,
p. 150.

[31]Larry Neal, "Investment Behavior by American Railroads," Op. Cit., p. 129.

[32]Melville Ulmer, Capital in Transportation, Op. Cit.,
p. 502.

Neal, one obtains the following pattern for the per cent of
total investment provided from retained earnings: 1880 to
1890 - 5%; 1893 to 1907 - 18%; and 1907 to 1916 - 39%. A
crude check of this procedure may be obtained by comparing
replacement costs from the retirement model for 1907 to
1916, 486 billion dollars, with Ulmer's depreciation reserve
figure for 1907 to 1916, 640 million dollars. The difference is in the expected direction and is generally consistent
with the average ratio of expenditures to reserve charges
reported by Neal - .49. The percentages produced by this
technique are admittedly imprecise, but the revised estimates do suggest that retained earnings accounted for an
increasing percentage of investment funds. In contrast to
Ulmer's figures the revised estimates indicate that this
trend received its major impetus in the period from 1893
to 1907.

Table 2.4 traces the ratio of funded debt to equity
over selected years from 1876 to 1914. Expansion through
1884 produced an increase in the debt-equity ratio, although
the increase is not as dramatic in the aggregate figures as
in the company data examined by Ripley.[33] Early finance was
largely accomplished by direct subscription to capital
stock, but speculative extension into undeveloped areas

---

[33]William Ripley, Railroads, Finance and Organization,
Op. Cit., pp. 30-1.

Table 2.4

RATIO OF BONDED DEBT TO EQUITY
(Selected Years 1876-1914)

Year	Ratio[a]
1876	.96
1884	.98
1893	1.12
1897	.98
1907	1.18
1914	1.33

[a]Funded debt and equity figures are from Bureau of
Census, Historical Statistics, Op. Cit., Series Q 35 and
Q 36, p. 428, and Series Q 98-100, p. 433. Equity includes
both preferred and common stock.

required access to the large Eastern and European money

markets which preferred bonded debt instruments. The ex-

tension after 1885 shows this pattern more clearly. The

increase in fixed interest payments as a result of specula-

tive extension increased the vulnerability of the sector to

the panic in 1893.

The recovery after 1897 was heavily financed from

bonded debt and an increase in preferred stock as a result

of the pattern of financing reorganizations, a desire to

avoid loss of control through equity purchases, and the

preference of large institutional investors for debt instru-

ments. In addition, a merger pattern developed in which the

parent company offered its own bonds in exchange for stock

in the merged company. This meant that the parent would
avoid subsequent new stock issues by the merged company,
since the parent would have to participate in such issues
to maintain control.[34]

External funds clearly remained the dominant source of
investment finance through 1914, although retained earnings
and replacement expenditures became increasingly important
after 1900. A steady increase in the ratio of debt to
equity was interrupted only by the crisis of 1893. Initially
this pattern resulted from the process of speculative expansion and a desire by financial sources to insure repayment.
After 1897 the trend was accelerated by the impact of financial institutions in the reorganization and consolidation
of the sector.

Summary

This brief summary of the major trends in the railroad
sector which impinged on investment behavior from 1870 to
1914 suggests that two factors were of dominant importance.
First it is clear that regional distinctions in investment
policy were significant. Main track extension into new
regions of the South and West was largely motivated by long
term expectations or construction profits and showed sharp
cyclical patterns. Cyclical increases in grain prices

---

[34]Ibid, pp. 110-1.

created high short term railroad profits and improved access
to bond and equity markets. The discontinuity of track
extension into new areas and the intense competition for
future monopoly positions combined to stimulate construction
which often exceeded the requirements of current demand.
Subsequent reversals in grain prices and related declines
in railroad profits reduced the ability of roads to meet
their fixed interest obligations and competition for available traffic became intense. Pooling agreements were ineffective in the face of strong cyclical pressures and the
ease of entry of new roads at reduced capitalization by
reorganizing defunct lines. Periodic crises and the poor
dividend record of railroads in this period are forceful
witnesses to this cyclical pattern. As demand increased
there were high returns to the creation of feeder lines,
auxiliary track, and rolling stock which stimulated a gradual
shift in the composition of capital. This latter trend was
most obvious on Northeastern and Middle Atlantic roads.

Second, the pattern of reorganization and consolidation of the sector after the crisis of 1893 produced an increased role of financial institutions in road management
and made further investment dependent on increased debt or
retained earnings. Retained earnings subsequently became
an important source of total investment funds increasing
from roughly five percent in 1880 to 1890 to almost forty

percent in 1907 to 1916. Similarly the debt to equity ratio increased dramatically from .98 in 1897 to 1.33 in 1914, producing a renewed burden of fixed interest payments on the sector.

Technical innovation and government control on the other hand had a limited impact on investment behavior in this period. The railroad sector was the pace setter for the economy in the rate of increasing output and total factor productivity, but the pace of innovation was quite constant and it is difficult to attribute any investment cycles to the dissemination of new techniques or equipment. The impact of government on investment behavior was also minimal until the end of the period. The Interstate Commerce Commission was largely limited to the role of unsuccessful plaintiff in initiating rate control cases prior to 1906, when the Hepburn Act provided the Commission with real regulatory power for the first time.

CHAPTER III

INVESTMENT THEORY AND THE RAILROAD SECTOR

Introduction

Reviewing the vast body of current literature on investment behavior, Robert Eisner graphically illustrated the plight of the theoretical entrepreneur.

> The rational (and informed) "entrepreneur," then, must plan a path for capital over time which maximizes his firm's present value, taking into account not only all of the initial conditions and current parameters - production function, supply and demand functions, and tax structure - but the expected values of these parameters over all the relevant future.[1]

It is unlikely that the resultant plan would assign constant weights to various economic indicators over extended periods of time. Summarizing the conflicting findings of various econometric estimates of theoretical models linking investment behavior to specific independent variables, Eisner concluded that "the word for today is humility."[2]

The investment decision is complex and is likely to depend on such varied factors as profit expectations, technological constraints, finance costs and the actions of

---

[1] Robert Eisner, "Investment and the Frustrations of Econometricians," American Economic Review (March 1969), p. 51.

[2] Ibid, p. 64.

rival firms. It is not surprising that numerous theories have arisen to explain the pattern of investment by a plethora of permutations and combinations of those potentially relevant variables. Time series or cross sections of data have been used to confront the theoretical formulations with conflicting results. A major problem with time series analysis is that investment behavior is not apt to be stable over long periods and short periods do not afford sufficient degrees of freedom for adequate statistical tests.

> Insofar as these series are composed of annual observations, it is absurd in all but the rarest instance to suppose that the qualitative content of the included variables has remained unchanged, or for that matter, the relative importance of included and excluded variables has remained invariant over time.[3]

Cross section analysis provides an expanded number of observations, but individual firm effects produce results which are not strictly comparable with time series analysis and "cross sections cannot be used successfully to make time series predictions unless a systematic relationship between the cross section and time series estimates has been firmly established."[4]

---

[3]John R. Meyer and Edwin Kuh, The Investment Decision (Cambridge: Harvard University Press, 1966), p. 54.

[4]Edwin Kuh, Capital Stock Growth: A Micro-Econometric Approach, Op. Cit., p. 186.

A detailed analysis of combined cross section and time series data would appear to be the logical solution to this dilemma. But the manipulation and statistical analysis of such large numbers of observations is a costly process, and for many purposes it would be preferable to use more aggregated data. Zvi Griliches and Yehuda Grunfeld concluded in their analysis of the use of such aggregated data that if the correlations between the error terms are negative, the macro-estimate would be superior to the summed micro-estimates for prediction.[5] But Thiel has also shown that aggregation almost always produces biased estimates of the structural coefficients.[6] Thus aggregate data is of limited value in distinguishing among competing investment theories where structural coefficients are important.

With these factors in mind it is clear that the investigator of investment behavior must proceed with caution. The following sections of this chapter pursue the relationship of the theory of investment behavior to the analysis of investment in the railroad sector. The first section provides a brief sketch of the relevant theory of investment. That sketch is followed by a summary of the findings of

---

[5]Zvi Griliches and Yehuda Grunfeld, "Is Aggregation Necessarily Bad?" Review of Economics and Statistics (January 1960).

[6]H. Thiel, Linear Aggregation of Economic Relations (Amsterdam: North Holland Publishing Co., 1954), p. 135.

former studies of investment in the railroad sector with emphasis on the period from 1870 to 1914. A final section compares the findings of those empirical studies with the qualitative record of the sector discussed in Chapter II.

Investment Theory

Investment theory has not enjoyed the elegance or empirical success that has fallen to consumer demand theory, a divergence which may be traced to the observation that there is no direct demand for investment in the sense that there is a direct demand for consumption. Rather there is a demand for a desired capital stock and the rate of investment depends on the deviation of the actual capital stock from the desired stock and the rate at which such deviations are corrected. Where investment projects continue for several periods this deviation may be defined in terms of the difference between the desired stock and the sum of the current stock plus uncompleted additions.

Theoretical content may be given to this relationship by assumptions on the variables determining the desired stock and the rate of adjustment. The traditional marginalist school centers on the role of interest rates, prices, and in some forms the expectation of future profits, while accelerator theories emphasize the relationship of demand to existing capacity. These theories have been modified by recent exploration of the impact of institutional constraints on the pattern of investment. To a considerable extent the institutional theories spring from the observation that management and ownership have become increasingly segregated and that decision rules, often related to risk aversion, are more important than in early theories where entrepreneurs held center stage. Eclectic theorists have stressed the shifting importance of different variables over the business cycle and the interaction of long and short term factors in determining investment fluctuations.

In the classic marginalist formulation the entrepreneur maximizes the discounted difference between the stream of revenues and costs generated by the purchase of a capital good. If all future returns and costs are known with certainty, technology is unchanged, and the rate of interest reflects the perceived cost of capital, the entrepreneur will purchase all capital goods with a positive present value. The volume of investment is uniquely determined by the price of capital and the rate of interest. Empirical testing of the marginalist theory has been largely unsuccessful but Dale Jorgenson attributes the negative findings to improper specification of the empirical tests. In his formulation the impact of interest and capital costs on a distributed lag of prior optimal capital stocks, rather than the relation of current investment to current interest and

prices, must be examined.[7] An interesting off-shoot of the
marginalist school has been the substitution of expectations
for known future returns. Tinbergen[8] and Klein[9] for example
have stressed the role of current profits in predicting
future returns, while Arrow explored the probability distribution of future profits and posited minimax behavior in
the face of uncertainty.[10]

The accelerator theories of investment center on the
hypothesis that changes in demand stimulate a change in the
desired level of capital in order to maintain the techno-
logically optimal ratio of capital to output. J. M. Clarke's
initial formulation of this model[11] has been modified to
allow for a desired level of excess capacity and a multi-
period rate of adjustment including decision lags and gestation periods.[12] If a desired level of excess capacity is

---

[7]Dale W. Jorgenson, "Capital Theory and Investment Behavior," American Economic Review (May 1963), pp. 247-259.

[8]Jan Tinbergen, Statistical Testing of Business Cycle
Theories, Op. Cit.

[9]Lawrence Klein, "Studies in Investment Behavior," Op.
Cit.

[10]Kenneth Arrow, "Alternative Approaches to the Theory
of Choice in Risk-taking Situations," Econometrica (October,
1951), pp. 404-437.

[11]J. M. Clark, "Business Acceleration and the Law of
Demand," Op. Cit.

[12]Hollis Chenery, "Overcapacity and the Acceleration
Principle," Econometrica (January 1952), pp. 1-28.

maintained a stock adjustment based on the level of output and the existing capital stock is more relevant than changes in the level of output. Although some models have employed profits rather than outputs as measures of demand, the accelerator hypothesis generally abstracts from financial costs and assumes that the availability of investable funds is not a constraint.

In recent years an "institutional" reaction to the mechanistic accelerator formulation has set in and new emphasis has been placed on financial restrictions. A major issue has been the interest elasticity of the supply of funds given the consistent finding of investment surveys that firms have an aversion to external finance as a result of managerial caution and that internal funds are therefore not valued at the market rate of interest.[13] If shifts in the supply and demand curves are synchronized, a strong possibility where both are related to profit levels, firms may habitually operate near the discontinuity in the supply curve between internal and external funds. Unusual opportunities or pressures may stimulate a resort to external finance but those factors would have little relation to fluctuations in

---

[13]James Duesenberry, Business Cycles and Economic Growth (New York: McGraw-Hill Book Co., 1958). Edwin Kuh and John Meyer, "Investment, Liquidity, and Monetary Policy," in Impacts of Monetary Policy, Commission on Money and Credit (Englewood Cliffs, N.J.: Prentice Hall, 1963).

the market rate of interest. Retained earnings should thus be a dominant factor in determining the rate of investment. In some models the proportion of earnings available for investment will be a function of a long run dividend policy and a sharp managerial aversion to dividend reduction.[14]

Meyer, Kuh and Glauber have argued that the importance of accelerator pressures and supply considerations vary over the business cycle.[15] Capacity-accelerator explanations do better on the up-swing when there is pressure on existing capacity, and residual funds explanations do better on the down-swing when emphasis is on research and the creation of excess capacity for future demand. In the short run investment is determined by a residual defined as profits minus established dividends. Capacity and accelerator pressures will determine deviations from the equality of the residual with desired investment, and market structure and oligopolistic market share competition will largely determine the rate at which investment responds to demand pressures. If this formulation is essentially valid one need search no further for an explanation of the difficulty of evaluating alternate theories of investment over extended periods of time

---

[14]John Lintner, "Dividends, Earnings, Leverage, Stock Prices and the Supply of Capital to Corporations," Review of Economics and Statistics (August, 1962), pp. 243-269.

[15]John Meyer and Edwin Kuh, The Investment Decision, Op. Cit.; John Meyer and Robert Glauber, Investment Decisions, Op. Cit.; Edwin Kuh, Capital Stock Growth, Op. Cit.

Empirical Tests of Investment Behavior in the Railroad Sector

The empirical tests of investment theory in the rail-road sector have largely been directed at testing specific hypotheses and the results have been quite mixed. Early studies by Kuznets (1935)[16] of the period from 1891 to 1930 and by Tinbergen (1938)[17] of the period from 1896 to 1913 generally verified J. M. Clarke's (1917)[18] accelerator hypothesis, although Tinbergen found a strong influence of profits and interest rates as well. All three studies sought to explain variations in new car orders as did Manne's (1945)[19] study of the period from 1897 to 1940. Manne corrected his data for the capacity of idle cars and obtained an accelerator coefficient which was closer to the theoretical level than his predecessors. On the other hand Eisner (1953)[20] examined variations in deflated gross investment

---

[16]Simon Kuznets, "Relation Between Capital Goods and Finished Products in the Business Cycle," in Economic Essays in Honour of Wesley Clair Mitchell (New York: 1935).

[17]Jan Tinbergen, Statistical Testing of Business Cycle Theories, Op. Cit.

[18]J. M. Clark, "Business Acceleration and the Law of Demand," Op. Cit.

[19]Alan S. Manne, "Some Notes on the Acceleration Principle," Review of Economics and Statistics (May, 1945), pp. 93-99.

[20]Robert Eisner, "Expectations, Plans and Capital Expenditures, A Synthesis of Ex Post and Ex Ante Data," cited in The Investment Decision, John Meyer and Edwin Kuh, Op. Cit., p. 31.

over a 1950 cross section of firms in utilities, transportation, and other non-manufacturing sectors and found little
support for the accelerator model.

Klein's (1951)[21] study of the sector drew on aggregate
estimates of gross investment for 1922 to 1941 derived by
the ICC[22] and cross section data for 1928, 1935 to 1937, and
1940. His principal findings were that: (1) both profits
and interest rates were important, (2) the capital stock had
a depressing effect on investment, (3) the investment pattern was more stable on a two-year than a one-year basis.
The most satisfactory results were obtained from the following time series model:[23]

$$I/p = 2647 + \underset{(9.8)}{.88} (NOR/p)_{-1} - \underset{(4.6)}{69} BOND\ R_{-1}$$

$$- \underset{(10.0)}{.20}\ K_{-1} - \underset{(2.3)}{301}\ p_{-1}$$

$$R^2 = .941$$

The symbols used throughout this study are summarized in
Table F2 but will be explained in the test as they are introduced. I represents annual gross investment in current

[21]Lawrence Klein, "Studies in Investment Behavior,"
Op. Cit.

[22]ICC, Bureau of Transport Economics and Statistics,
Post-war Capital Expenditures of the Railroads (Washington:
GPO, 1947), p. 35.

[23]Lawrence Klein, "Studies in Investment Behavior,"
Op. Cit., pp. 250, 253, 255-256, 272.

dollars, p is a capital goods price index, NOR is net operating revenue, BOND R is the railroad bond rate, and K is the
gross capital stock. The numbers in parentheses under the
coefficients represent the "t" statistic, a convention which
is continued throughout the text to facilitate interpretation of the results. In general a "t" statistic greater
than 2.0 implies that the null hypothesis that the coefficient is different from zero cannot be rejected at the ninety-
five percent confidence level, although the precise cut-off
value depends on the number of degrees of freedom.

In a comprehensive analysis of former econometric
studies of investment behavior Eisner and Strotz (1963)[24]
renewed a criticism of Klein's analysis first made by
Leontief (1951)[25] that Klein's formulation is very similar
to a stock adjustment model if profits are taken as a proxy
for output. This observation, coupled with contradictory
results for the role of interest rates depending on the precise specification of the model, casts some question on the
interpretation of Klein's work. It is clear that profits
played an important role in his model, but the interpretation

---

[24]Robert Eisner and R. H. Strotz, "Determinants of
Business Investment," in Impacts of Monetary Policy, Com-
mission on Money and Credit (Englewood Cliffs, N.J.:
Prentice Hall, 1963), p. 148.

[25]Wassily Leontief, "Comment," in Conference on Business Cycles (New York: NBER, 1951), pp. 310-311.

that profits reflected future profitability rather than output pressures is questionable.

Koyck's (1954)[26] analysis of investment in freight cars
over the period from 1894 to 1940 had a strong influence on
future analysis of the accelerator principle. In his model
current investment is related to a distributed lag of past
income changes plus a trend variable. By assuming that coefficients of the lagged income changes after the second
year were related by multiples of a single constant he was
able to estimate the equation using only four unknown coefficients. But his important contribution was the emphasis
on the gradual adjustment of investment to changes in income.
Of particular interest is his observation that adjustments
proceeded very rapidly in the "expansionary period" from
1894 to 1915 and much less rapidly in the period from 1920
to 1939 because of the reduced excess capacity of the earlier
period. Thus the interval of J. M. Clarke's initial analysis
of the simple accelerator was the most favorable period for
his theory.[27]

Kmenta and Williamson sought to "isolate the likely
changes in investment behavior which occur as the industry
passes through a fairly predictable set of institutional and

---

[26]L. M. Koyck, Distributed Lags and Investment Analysis
(Amsterdam: North Holland Publishing Co., 1954).

[27]Ibid, p. 109.

growth phases" in analyzing the railroad sector over the period from 1872 to 1941.[28] They proposed separate models for the period of "adolescence" from 1872 to 1895, "maturity" from 1896 to 1914, and "senility" from 1922 to 1941. The adolescence model combines a profit accelerator and the ratio of profits to capital to explain the entry of new firms and a stock adjustment to explain investment by existing firms. The stock adjustment model assumes that roads operated with a capital stock they considered optimal for present demand, and that they perceived that changes in demand would be permanent. Two year lags are used in the adolescence model due to "inefficient communications systems, administrative procedures, and capital raising methods" and the long gestation period of new investment.[29] The maturity model is a simple stock adjustment with a two year lag. Profit levels and changes are omitted because entry became more restricted in the face of the merger movement. In the senility model investment is perceived as replacing worn equipment with technically superior capital and there is a sharp aversion to external finance. The model thus contains only lagged capital and profits, the latter now measuring the availability of funds rather than profit expectations. The models and results obtained by Kmenta and Williamson

---

[28]Jan Kmenta and Jeffrey Williamson, Op. Cit., p. 172.
[29]Ibid, p. 176.

are as follows:

Adolescence, 1873-1895

$$I^N = 697 + 1.03 \underset{(3.8)}{X}_{-2} - .24 \underset{(4.8)}{K^N}_{-2}$$
$$ (1.8)$$

$$+ 278.3 \ \frac{(NOR/p)}{K^N}_{-2} + 2.0 \ (DNOR/p)_{-1}$$
$$ (6.7) \phantom{\frac{(NOR/p)}{K^N}} (3.0)$$

$$R^2 = .807$$

Maturity, 1896-1914

$$I^N = 778 + .42 \underset{(4.7)}{X}_{-2} - .10 \underset{(2.5)}{K^N}_{-2}$$
$$ (1.6)$$

$$R^2 = .821$$

Senility, 1922-1941

$$I^N = 3344 - .16 \ K^N_{-1} + .71 \ (NR/p)_{-1}$$

$$R^2 = .898$$

Once again the parentheses under the coefficients refer to
the "t" statistics. The superscript N refers to net values
and the prefix D refers to the first difference. X is a
link relative output index and NR refers to net revenue from
all sources.

All of the Kmenta and Williamson models omit any
measures of interest rates or equity yields. In the first
period this is defended by disequilibrium conditions where
"the long run marginal efficiency of the last project

exceeds the interest rate by a considerable margin,"[30] and
in the last period the omission is justified by a reluctance
or difficulty of firms to obtain external finance. No men-
tion of interest rates is made for the period of maturity.
Kmenta and Williamson tested their models against new estimates of Klein's general model cited above for each period
using Ulmer's capital and investment data. In each case
their own models performed best in the period for which they
were designed. Their tests of Klein's model produced positive and generally insignificant coefficients for the
interest variable in every period including the interval of
Klein's initial analysis - 1922 to 1941.

The overriding weakness of the Kmenta and Williamson
study is its reliance on the Ulmer data for the period prior
to 1914. They were aware of Fishlow's criticism of the
trend and annual variation of those capital and investment
series but decided it was "unduly cautious to abstain from
using this wealth of historical information while awaiting
future revisions."[31] More caution was warranted. My independent estimates of capital and investment derived in
Appendix D differ sharply from Ulmer's estimates for the
period from 1872 to 1914. In light of this discrepancy
there is little point in pursuing the detailed statistical

---

[30] Ibid, p. 177.
[31] Ibid, p. 172.

results obtained by Kmenta and Williamson, but three points on the specification of their models may be raised. First the use of the level and rate of change of profits with a two year lag as a measure of stimulus to new firm entry in the period from 1872 to 1895 is questionable. The gestation period for new roads was certainly longer than two years in this interval, even after the decision to invest had been reached and the charter obtained. Coupling the physical constraints of survey and construction with any reasonable decision period the two year lag is clearly inappropriate. Second the assumption that firms adjusted their capital stocks to demand pressures in the period from 1872 to 1895 is tenuous. Auxiliary track and equipment investment probably was geared to increasing demand, but main track extension which accounted for the vast majority of investment in this period was generally linked to long term considerations only partially explained by current demand. Finally the omission of any measure of the cost of external finance in the period from 1896 to 1914 is surprising. There was a clear easing of credit conditions in the recovery after 1898 reflected by a period of low bond rates and equity yields from 1899 to 1907,[32] and it is questionable that a simple stock adjustment which abstracts from changes in the cost of finance would best explain investment in this period.

---

[32]Table F1.

The latter point was the major thrust of Neal's criticism of the Kmenta and Williamson analysis. Using revised
estimates of capital and investment based on a sample of
21 companies scaled by mileage of road operated, Neal found
that "investment behavior in the period 1897 to 1914 is best
understood by emphasizing the role of financial factors."[33]
Neal's capital and investment estimates are very similar to
those I derived by an alternate technique in Appendix D and
seem to correct the shortcomings of Ulmer's data. Neal
tested the Kmenta and Williamson models for the period from
1897 to 1914 and found that none of them worked particularly
well and that the maturity model performed worst in this
period for which it was developed. He examined four additional models including the Klein model cited above, an
adaptation of Eisner's distributed lag of prior changes in
sales,[34] the Jorgenson neoclassical model,[35] and a financial
model containing lagged outputs, retained earnings and equity
yields.

Tests of the financial model for 1897 to 1914 produced
the following result:

---

[33]Larry Neal, "Investment Behavior by American Railroads, 1897-1914," Op. Cit., p. 126.

[34]Robert Eisner, "A Distributed Lag Investment Function," Econometrica (January, 1960), pp. 1-29.

[35]Dale Jorgenson, "Capital Theory and Investment Behavior," American Economic Review (May, 1963), pp. 247-259.

$$I = 245 + \underset{(9.1)}{.436} X_{-1} + \underset{(3.9)}{.97} RETE_{-1} - \underset{(3.4)}{150} EQ\ YLD_{-1}$$

$$R^2 = .87$$

RETE is retained earnings and EQ YLD is the equity yield.
Neal repeated the test for the period 1897 to 1907 omitting
the retained earnings variable to demonstrate that the equity
yield and output were most important in this period of eased
financing costs and obtained the following result:

$$I = 68.4 + \underset{(21.7)}{.587} X_{-1} - \underset{(4.4)}{142.68} EQ\ YLD_{-1}$$

$$R^2 = .98$$

These results were superior to those for the other models
tested but were comparable to the results for the Eisner
distributed lag model which abstracts from financial changes.
Neal examined the latter model for the period from 1898 to
1907 and found that the reaction coefficients were higher
than for the period 1898 to 1914 and that the coefficient
on lagged investment had similarly increased. He concluded
that the results showed a more rapid process of adjustment
in the period of financial ease. Finally his test of the
Klein model produced good results, and the interest coefficient was properly negative and significant.

Neal's reliance on revised capital and investment data
is encouraging and his principal finding that investment behavior was modified by changing financial conditions is
generally established. However there are three points which

make the comparison of his results for different models questionable. First, his financial model purports to explain gross investment without reference to the capital stock, but this is equivalent to assuming that all capital adjustments are completed in one period and that replacement expenditures are not a function of the existing level of the capital stock and its age distribution.[36] Second, the capital stock coefficient is insignificant in every model in which it appears including the distributed lag accelerator. This makes Neal's interpretation of changes in the reaction coefficients tenuous. Finally the size of Neal's samples, the smallest having 11 observations and the largest 18, raises the usual questions on the small sample properties of least squares estimation.

Summary

Prior studies of investment behavior in the railroad sector have largely centered on the testing of alternate theoretical concepts, but as Eisner and Strotz note the real problem is not to accept or reject hypotheses but to weigh the relative impacts of various factors.

> The real problem is to assess the magnitudes of the effects of changes in sales, in profits, in interest rates, in prices, and thus to acquire genuine quantitative information. But our data and our

---

[36] Zvi Griliches, "Capital Stock in Investment Functions," in Measurement in Economics, Carl Christ et. al. (Stanford: Stanford University Press, 1963), p. 116.

statistical techniques will not bear the weight. We
are reduced instead to classifying explanatory variables: important or unimportant.[37]

Even by this weak criterion the results of empirical tests

in the sector are mixed.

Most of the early studies examined variations in new

car orders and concluded that accelerator pressures were im-

portant, and Koyck's analysis suggested that they were

particularly important in the period from 1894 to 1915.

Studies of aggregate capital and investment data by Klein

for 1922 to 1941 and by Neal for 1897 to 1914 indicated that

retained earnings or profits and interest rates were equally

important. For the earlier period back to 1870 only the

study of aggregate data by Kmenta and Williamson is avail-

able. Their analysis suffers from a reliance on question-

able investment data as well as problems of model specifica-

tion.

The distinction between studies of total aggregate

investment and of equipment alone is important, since it is

very likely that investment behavior differed for various

capital components. In particular one would expect that

main track extension would be a function of long range plan-

ning based on expectations of regional growth and the main-

tenance of a strong market share position. Investment in

---

[37]Robert Eisner and R. H. Strotz, "Determinants of
Business Investment," Op. Cit., p. 233.

equipment and auxiliary track should be more related to current demand conditions, particularly when the increasing
returns to scale resulting from the discontinuities of main
track extension and subsequent market growth are considered.
These compositional distinctions would be further reflected
in disparities in regional investment behavior given the
pattern of territorial expansion in the West and intensive
response to growing markets in the East.

The qualitative record of expansion thus suggests sharp
disparities in investment behavior over different regions
and for different capital components. The use of aggregate
data which abstracts from these important distinctions will
quite likely distort important investment patterns. Moreover an emphasis on the age of the industry as a whole in
determining changing investment behavior may well direct
attention to unimportant issues. In particular the reorganization of capital markets around 1900 had a major impact
on investment behavior, but emphasis on life cycle considerations led Kmenta and Williamson to omit financial factors
from their model for that period.

This analysis of prior studies of the sector in the
period from 1870 to 1914 failed to produce a consistent
basis for evaluating changing investment behavior. Flashes
of insight have been provided but statistical verification
has been too tenuous to establish any but the most general

propositions. However the analysis of those studies has in-

dicated that further emphasis should be placed on obtaining

precise measures of capital, increasing the number of

degrees of freedom for statistical testing, examining in-

vestment behavior by capital components over different

regions, and testing various formulations of theoretical

models to establish the sensitivity of the results to alter-

nate specifications.

CHAPTER IV

EMPIRICAL RESULTS: AGGREGATE DATA

Introduction

Previous discussion has suggested that the use of aggregate data to examine investment behavior in the railroad sector from 1870 to 1914 could easily lead to a distorted picture of investment patterns. First, one would expect major disparities in behavior in different regions and for different capital components. Second, the use of aggregate data over short time periods does not supply sufficient degrees of freedom for adequate statistical testing. Finally, the use of various measures of capital and investment in different prior studies has made the analysis of changing behavior over time difficult.

This chapter attempts to correct these deficiencies as far as possible by providing a standard with which subsequent cross section and company time series results may be compared. Total investment analysis is supplemented by separate examinations of investment in equipment and in track. The results are presented for the entire period from 1870 to 1914, and compared with findings for 1870 to 1895 and 1895 to 1914. New aggregate gross investment, gross capital, output, earnings, and price series were derived in

order to provide a consistent data base with which to examine investment patterns. The construction of those series
is discussed briefly in the text but detailed accounts are
provided in separate appendixes. The method of deriving the
aggregate investment and capital series was also applied to
subsequent derivations for individual companies so that statistical results for comparable data could be examined.

The first section discusses the data employed in subsequent statistical analysis with emphasis on the capital
and investment estimates. The second section compares the
findings of regression tests of models from former studies
using the new total investment data with the findings of
other investigators. In the third section the results for
those models for different components of capital and periods
are compared in some detail with emphasis on isolating
changes in investment behavior. The fourth section briefly
reports the results of additional tests used to clarify the
observed statistical pattern.

Data

Table F1 contains all of the aggregate data used in the
regression tests cited in this chapter. Special note will
be made of the role of investment, capital, price, output,
capacity pressure, and lagged investment variables.

Investment. - - When investment theory is to be confronted with empirical analysis a major question emerges

over the relevant concepts of capital and investment. Gross
investment may be defined as capital replacements plus net
capital additions, and net investment estimates are habitually derived by subtracting capital replacements from this
gross figure. However it is difficult to distinguish between
net additions and replacements with empirical data, because
of technical changes in the capital goods. Depreciation
rates to determine replacement requirements have almost
universally been based on the rate of reduction in the market
value of capital goods. The decline in market value may be
interpreted as the decline in the discounted value of all
future services the capital goods will contribute and is
therefore a composite of exhaustion (reduced calendar life),
deterioration (less productive life), and obsolescence or
"homicide to make room for a favorite rather than natural
death."[1] But if the entrepreneur invests to maintain or
increase the current level of capacity, as implied by the
accelerator theory, only deterioration of the capital stock
is relevant.

Under these conditions the use of the decline in market
value to determine depreciation is not appropriate. Net investment should be determined from detailed information on
the pattern of capital deterioration over time. If such

---

[1]Tibor Barna, "On Measuring Capital," in The Theory of
Capital, F. A. Lutz ed. (London: MacMillan and Co., 1963),
p. 85.

information is not available or if there is no evidence of significant deterioration over the life of capital, gross investment is, a more appealing dependent variable. In order to avoid the distorting impact of a questionable depreciation scheme on the dependent variable, gross investment is used in subsequent analysis. Gross investment also corresponds to the output of the capital goods sector and has traditionally played a central role in business cycle theory. Appendix D traces the derivation of the estimates of gross investment in current dollars by applying new estimates of annual prices of the principal components of capital to annual component purchases. The gross investment figures shown in Table F1 by component thus measure "out of pocket" expenditures on roughly eighty percent of all capital goods as discussed in Appendix D.

Capital. - - Where all deviations of the capital stock from the desired level are not corrected in one period, the level of gross investment must reflect the history of previous additions to capital as measured by a capital stock variable in some form. If the contribution of services does not deteriorate over the life of capital, the "one-horse shay" assumption, gross capital computed by average life replacement is an appropriate measure of capital capacity. In many cases this assumption is superior to straight line or declining balance depreciation schemes based on changes

in value rather than service contribution. Various capital
components in either case should be weighted by their relative contributions to current output to obtain a consistent
measure of the flow of capital services. Durability distinctions are meaningless when applied to capital as a factor of
production.[2]

The appropriate measure of capital then must account
for the changing contribution to production of each capital
component over time. Appendix E derives indexes of the
changing efficiency of track, locomotives, passenger cars,
and freight cars over the period from 1870 to 1914. Those
indexes are applied to estimated purchases and retirements
of each capital component in Appendix D to obtain series of
gross annual additions of each component in 1910 efficiency
units. A single capital series is derived by applying 1910
prices to each component series and summing over all components. Assuming that the contribution of each component
to current production did not decline significantly over its
average life, the resultant gross capital series in 1910
dollars provides a consistent estimate of capital measured
by its capacity rather than its cost.

In his study of economic growth in the entire United
States economy Edward Denison observed that it would be

---

[2]Trygve Haavelmo, A Study in the Theory of Investment
(Chicago: Chicago University Press, 1961), p. 93.

impossible to implement a constant dollar capital series
such as the one outlined above which would "equate capital
goods produced at different times by their ability to contribute to production, taking full account of their capacity,
operating costs . . . quality of product, and other aspects
of performance."[3] In emphasizing that an improvement in
society's ability to use the resource should not be interpreted as an increase in the quality or quantity of the
capital good, he proposed an alternate constant dollar
measure of the capital stock.

> The value, in base period prices, of the stock of
> durable capital goods (before allowance for capital
> consumption) measures the amount it would have cost
> in the base period to produce the actual stock of
> capital goods existing in the given year (not its
> equivalent ability to contribute to production).[4]

This latter position was also adopted by Albert Fishlow when
he observed:

> The principle involved is clear. Each physical
> unit, whether of track or equipment, should be
> weighted by its cost of reproduction in the prices
> and technology of a given year before being com-
> pared. In this way one gets a consistent measure
> of the capital stock over time, where real invest-
> ment is measured, as is conventional, by its cost,
> not its capacity.[5]

---

[3]Edward Denison, The Sources of Economic Growth in the
United States and the Alternatives Before Us, Supplementary
Paper No. 13 (Committee for Economic Development, 1962), p.
86.

[4]Ibid, pp. 94-5.

[5]Albert Fishlow, "Productivity and Technological
Change," Op. Cit., p. 595.

This technique does indeed produce a consistent measure of the capital stock in dollars of the base year. For some purposes such a measure may be useful if subsequent analysis takes account of changing capital efficiency over time. But for an analysis of investment decisions it is essential that capital be measured by its productive capacity and hence corrections for relative efficiency rather than relative reproduction costs are required. Further it is not at all clear that reproduction costs are easier to obtain than relative efficiency measures, since reproduction cost estimates generally depend upon hypothetical production functions for many items that were not produced in the base year. Where actual decisions are to be examined it is preferable to relate investment to observable price and efficiency relationships.

The most common alternative to either of these measures of the capital stock is the deflation of annual investment expenditures by a capital price index, and the application of these annual changes to some base estimate of the capital stock. The resultant capital stock is referred to as a "constant dollar" measure but this is usually a wishful misnomer. The interpretation of such a series is not clear where technological change has produced new commodities which are no longer comparable to early vintages. The capital stock is measured by its value in base period prices assuming that current prices refer to comparable commodities, but when the commodities are not comparable the capital series will distort changes in capital measured by its capacity.

Price Index. - - Regression analysis rests on the assumption that the available data reflect some constant relationship of the dependent variable with specified explanatory variables. In the case of investment analysis it is clear that railroad entrepreneurs develop their investment programs in terms of current dollars values. Capital capacity on the other hand will be considered in terms of efficiency units in constant dollar terms. If other current dollar terms are introduced in the regression model without correcting for price variations over time, least squares estimates will reflect a spurious correlation between the dependent variable and other current dollar variables. In such cases some measure of price changes should be introduced explicitly as an independent variable, or all the variables should be expressed in constant dollar terms. Since the behavioral relation centers on investment in current dollar terms it is preferable to introduce a price variable explicitly.

Appendix C derives a railroad capital goods price index with a 1910 base for the period from 1870 to 1914. Efficiency adjustments from Appendix E are applied to current prices in the index to develop price estimates for comparable commodities. The use of a 1910 base produces some distortion in the early period from 1870 to 1880 because of the low weight applied to the rail price series, but regression analysis discussed in Appendix C suggested that no change in the statistical results would occur if an 1870 base were used instead, since the annual variation of the series was so similar. There were no significant base problems for separate equipment and track price indexes.

Output and Earnings. - - A link relative output index for the period from 1870 to 1914 is derived in Appendix A by extending the results of other studies back to 1870 with reference to output and rate estimates from a fifteen company sample. Similarly gross and net operating revenue estimates were produced to correct discrepancies in the coverage of series prior to 1890. Output estimates are reported in 1910 dollars since they refer to weighted physical quantities while revenue data were left in current dollar terms.

Capacity Pressure. - - A capacity pressure variable was defined as the product of current output and the minimum prior ratio of gross capital to output. Assuming that the minimum prior capital-output ratio reflected the level of optimal capacity utilization, the capacity pressure variable should be a meaningful measure of technological expansionary pressure. In effect this variable provides a method of correcting for excess capital capacity and constrains the sign of the capital coefficient to negative values.

Lagged Investment. - - Various interpretations may be placed on the role of lagged investment as an independent variable. One of the most cogent arguments is that investment programs develop an institutional momentum which makes it difficult to alter an established rate of investment.[6] An alternate, widely cited, argument for the inclusion of lagged investment is that current expenditures are a function of a broad range of prior values of the explanatory variables rather than their current values alone. This position is particularly applicable to models based on expectations which are related to prior experience or which specify gradual adjustment processes. The lagged investment variable in effect serves to transform the model into a distributed lag of all the other independent variables, and conserves the available statistical degrees of freedom since the parameters of the distributed lag need not be estimated.[7] On the other hand the use of a lagged dependent variable as an independent variable biases the normal Durbin-Watson test for autocorrelation, and thus creates problems

---

[6]John Meyer and Robert Glauber, Investment Decisions, Op. Cit., p. 27.

[7]L. M. Koyck, Distributed Lags and Investment Analysis, Op. Cit., Chapter 2.

in comparing the results with other models. Further if
serial correlation of the error terms is present the ordinary least squares estimates will be inconsistent, that
is increasing the sample size will not necessarily make the
coefficient estimates converge on their "true" values.
Thus the inclusion of lagged investment is often desireable
in terms of the theoretical model structure, but the statistical results must be interpreted with care.

Tests of Models from Prior Studies
with Revised Aggregate Data

Table F3 presents the aggregate models which are discussed in this section using the variable symbols defined
in Table F2. Model 1-1 is taken from Klein, Model 1-2 is
Neal's financial model, Model 1-3 is Neal's reduced version
of Eisner's distributed lag accelerator, and Models 1-4,
1-5, and 1-6 are Kmenta and Williamson's adolescence,
maturity, and senility models respectively.[8] The prefix
"1" on the model designations indicates an aggregate model,
while prefixes "3" and "2" introduced in Chapters V and VI
refer to cross section and company time series models respectively. The ordinary least squares estimates in Table
F3 are presented for total, track, and equipment investment
in the periods 1872-1895 and 1896-1914. The parentheses
again enclose the "t" statistic for each estimated

[8]See Chapter III.

coefficient. This section will examine only the results for total investment (subscripts "a" and "b" in Table F3) and compare them with the corresponding findings of other investigators.

Model 1-1. - - The results for Klein's general model in the period from 1896 to 1914 are comparable with his estimates for 1922 to 1941 and with Neal's estimates for the period 1897 to 1914. There is no evidence of autocorrelation and the model explains a high proportion of investment variance. The capital and price coefficients have the appropriate signs but are marginally insignificant, and the interest rate and profits have the appropriate signs and are significant. The model is less impressive in the period from 1872 to 1895 and there is evidence of autocorrelation, but all coefficients again have the correct signs and only the profit coefficient is not significant. Of special note is the strong negative coefficient for the interest rate in both periods, a finding which is at variance with the Kmenta and Williamson result that the interest coefficients in these periods were positive and insignificant.

Model 1-2. - - Neal's financial model produced impressive results in the period 1896-1914 which were very similar to his findings. All of the coefficients were significant and the R^2 was quite high. The model structure broke down in the period 1872-1895 when there was also evidence of

autocorrelation. The shift in model structure is significant, especially in the coefficients for output and equity
yield, and suggests that there was a substantial increase
in the significance of those factors in the later period.

Model 1-3. - - The estimates for the modified Eisner
distributed lag accelerator are again very close to those
obtained by Neal for the period 1896-1914, although the R^2
of .78 is significantly lower than his .90. The capital
coefficient is insignificant, but all the other coefficients
are highly significant and have the correct signs. The
model structure breaks down in the period from 1872 to
1895 and only the coefficient of lagged investment is significant. Further, there are indications of autocorrelation
in the early period and, since a lagged dependent variable
is used as an independent variable, this suggests that the
coefficient estimates are not efficient.

Model 1-4. - - The Kmenta and Williamson adolescence
model performs poorly in both periods and produces low
squared correlation coefficients. In the period for which
it was designed, 1872-1895, only capital and net operating
revenue are significant with the correct signs. The ratio
of net operating revenue to capital is significant but has
a negative coefficient. None of the variables is significant in the period 1896-1914.

Model 1-5. - - The Kmenta and Williamson maturity model also does very poorly in both periods. None of the coefficients is significant in either period and the R^2s are low. The sign structure is correct for the early period, but reverses in the period from 1896-1914 for which the model was designed.

Model 1-6. - - The Kmenta and Williamson senility model produces reasonable results for the period from 1896-1914 with appropriate signs and significant coefficients. The R^2 of .55 is low compared to alternate models but is the highest obtained by any of the life-cycle specifications. The model breaks down in the period from 1870 to 1895 and no coefficients are significant.

None of the models tested explained investment in the period from 1870 to 1895 particularly well. The Klein general model (1-1) had the most satisfactory coefficient structure and the highest R^2 for that period but also showed signs of autocorrelation. The coefficient structure broke down in every other model tested and the explained variance was uniformly low. The results for 1896 to 1914 were much better. The Klein model (1-1) and Neal's finance (1-2) and distributed lag (1-3) formulations all produced the correct a priori coefficient structure and explained a high proportion of the variance. In contrast to Neal's findings, the distributed lag model (1-3) had a lower R^2 than the Klein

general model (1-1) and the Real finance model (1-2). All
of the Kmenta and Williamson models produced poor results
in terms of coefficient structure and R^2s with the exception
of the senility model for the period 1896-1914. In terms of
the coefficient structure none of the life cycle models performed best in the period for which it was designed.

Comparison of Results by Component and Period

To explore the impact of investment behavior for separate capital components the six models cited above were examined using investment in track and in equipment as dependent
variables. Capital and price data used in those models corresponded to the component being tested. Table F3 again
reports the detailed results of those tests for the periods
1872-1895 and 1896-1914. The coefficient structure of the
models is perhaps the most important touchstone of comparison but to simplify the presentation of the results the R^2,
corrected for the number of degrees of freedom, from each
model is reported in Table 4.1. The R^2 for tests of each
model for the entire period from 1872 to 1914 is given as
well.

Examining Table 4.1 it is clear that division of the
entire period into two sub-periods increases the explanatory
power of every model of total and track investment. But for
equipment investment there is a tendency for the early
period R^2 to fall and the later period R^2 to increase

Table 4.1

COMPARISON OF AGGREGATE MODEL SQUARED CORRELATION COEFFICIENTS

Model	Period	R^2 by Component		
		Total	Track	Equipment
1-1	1872-1914	.53	.39	.41
	1872-1895	.64	.59	.34
	1896-1914	.87	.67	.81
1-2	1872-1914	.21	.07	.58
	1872-1895	.42	.47	.13
	1896-1914	.80	.62	.83
1-3	1872-1914	.56	.23	.68
	1872-1895	.46	.38	.21
	1896-1914	.78	.59	.88
1-4	1872-1914	.15	.15	.10
	1872-1895	.32	.28	.19
	1896-1914	.40	.47	.36
1-5	1872-1914	.14	.14	.07
	1872-1895	.13	.24	.11
	1896-1914	.30	.22	.33
1-6	1872-1914	.02	.01	.14
	1872-1895	.05	.08	.04
	1896-1914	.55	.08	.35

Column	Description
Model	Model designations are explained in the notes to Table F3.
R^2	The R^2 listed is adjusted for the number of degrees of freedom.

compared with the results for the entire period, as illustrated in Models 1-1, 1-2, 1-3, and 1-6. In every model of total, track, or equipment investment but two the period division produces a higher R^2 for 1896-1914 than for 1872-1895, the exceptions being a tie for equipment model 1-6 and a small decline in track model 1-5. Thus the hypothesis that investment behavior changed between the two periods is supported, but all of the models appear to work better in the later period.

The division of total investment into two components does not produce the same effect. In half the cases the R^2 for total investment was higher than the R^2 for each component and in no case were the R^2s of both components higher than for total investment. One striking pattern does appear. The R^2 for all models is higher for track than equipment in the period from 1872 to 1895, and is higher for equipment than track in the period from 1896 to 1914 for all models but 1-4. Thus the examination of investment in separate components does not provide the sharp improvement in results which was expected, but it does indicate that the models work best for track in the early period and for equipment in the later period.

A preliminary view of model performance from Table 4.1 suggests that the Klein general model (1-1) consistently produces the best or second best results for total and track

investment in all periods. The modified Eisner distributed
lag accelerator model (1-3) works best for equipment investment in 1896-1914 although the Neal finance model (1-2) is
a close second, and the inclusion of lagged investment in
the Eisner model prevents the results from being strictly
comparable. None of the models work well for equipment investment from 1872-1895, the best results being obtained from
the Klein model (1-1) with an R^2 of .339. The financial
models (1-1 and 1-2) work best in the period from 1896-1914,
a result which supports Neal's basic contention, but surprisingly the R^2s are higher for equipment than track investment. The distributed lag model (1-3) also produces
much better results for equipment than track investment in
the period 1896-1914.

This preliminary analysis of model performance based
on the R^2 is generally supported by a detailed analysis of
changing coefficient structure from Table F3, although a few
clarifications are required. Although the R^2 of the Klein
(1-1) track model increases in the latter period only the
bond rate remains significant. The bond rate is less important in the Klein equipment model which shows an increasing significance for profits in the later period. The increasing importance of financial factors is clearly shown
in the Neal financial model (1-2). Only retained earnings
is significant in the 1872-1895 period in the track model

and none of the coefficients of the equipment model is significant. In sharp contrast the 1896-1914 equipment model has all highly significant coefficients, and in the track model only the retained earnings coefficient is not significant. The Neal distributed lag accelerator model (1-3) has poor coefficient structure except for equipment from 1896-1914 where all of the coefficients but capital are highly significant and the explanatory power increases dramatically. An examination of the coefficient structure of the models thus supports the argument that financial factors became more important in the later period and underscores the strong performance of the distributed lag accelerator in explaining investment in equipment in that period.

The Kmenta and Williamson models fare no better for separate components than they did for total investment. The limited explanatory power of their models rested primarily on the retarding effect of capital and the positive impact of profits, although the capital coefficient was significant in only three of the eight model versions and profits in five of eight. The pattern of changing coefficient structure thus underscores the increasing importance of financial factors after 1895 with a primary impact on equipment investment, the improved performance of the distributed lag accelerator model for equipment after 1895, the weak performance of all models prior to 1895 with the

possible exception of the Klein track model, and the poor
performance of the stage of growth models.

Further Explorations with Aggregate Data

In order to clarify the results of the preceding section and test their sensitivity to specific model formulations several additional models were examined. Particular
emphasis was placed on different forms of the dependent
variable, various lag formulations, and the impact of intro-
ducing specific variables in the same equation. In addition
a detailed residual analysis was performed for a distributed
lag accelerator, a simple stock adjustment model, and Klein's
general model which appeared to produce the best overall
results in the last section.

Several models were examined using the variables in
annual, two year average, and first difference specifications. The two year average form consistently produced the
best results supporting Klein's contention that, "it is
entirely possible that the anatomy of investment decisions
will become clear only from data taken from periods longer
than one year."[9] The first difference form consistently
produced the weakest overall results.

The examination of lag structures produced less deci-
sive conclusions. In particular stock adjustment models

---

[9]Lawrence Klein, "Studies in Investment Behavior," Op.
Cit., p. 242.

were examined to see if the Kmenta and Williamson hypothesis
of a two year lag structure in the periods 1872-1895 and
1896-1914 was appropriate. With only lagged capital and
output in the equation a one year lag produced the best results for total investment in both periods. When lagged
investment was also introduced into the equation a one year
lag was still superior in the early period, but a two year
lag was better in the later period. For the entire period
1872-1914 a one year lag produced the best results in both
models. Thus while the results are mixed a one year lag
seems most appropriate in both periods.

Tests of other models performed by stepping in variables to examine their impact on the estimated equation
produced three consistent findings on the impact of specific
variables. 1) Net operating revenue and output were too
closely correlated with each other to include them in the
same equation, a finding which suggests that it is difficult
to distinguish between the role of profits and output with
aggregate data. 2) The bond rate and equity yield were also
highly correlated with each other and produced poor results
when included in the same equation. The results for separate bond rate and equity yield models were significantly
improved when the price index was also included. 3) The
capacity pressure variable, defined as the minimum prior

ratio of gross capital to output multiplied by current output, consistently produced very weak results.

Finally a graphical analysis of ordinary least squares
regression residuals was performed for three models: (1) the
modified Eisner distributed lag accelerator, (2) a stock
adjustment model using lagged investment, net operating
revenue, and capital, (3) the Klein general model. In each
case total gross investment was used as the dependent variable and regressions were run for the periods 1872-1895,
1896-1914, and 1872-1914. The distributed lag accelerator
performed very well over the smooth investment cycles from
1873-1892 and 1906-1914, but in periods of more rapid fluctuation the model tended to over correct and often missed
cyclical turning points. In the early period the predicted
series tended to lag the actual series slightly and under-
estimated the actual peaks. The stock adjustment model
smooths through the actual variations from 1873-1892 falling
short of the peaks and remaining above the troughs. Like
the distributed lag accelerator, the stock adjustment model
tended to smooth through sharp cyclical variations and performed poorly in the periods 1893-1898 and 1906-1914, although it traced the smoother expansion from 1898 to 1905
quite well. Klein's model performed very much like the
stock adjustment model from 1873-1892 but was much more
efficient at catching the subsequent sharp variations from

1892-1898 and traced the variations from 1898 to 1914 quite closely. The superior performance of the Klein general model thus appears to rest on its bifurcated role in different cyclical periods. The inclusion of financial factors accounts for its improved cyclical performance after 1895, while profits also act as a proxy for output in establishing long trends via a stock adjustment mechanism.

This brief analysis of a number of supplementary tests thus partially clarifies the original findings for prior aggregate models. In particular it is difficult to distinguish between the roles of profits and output when they are included in a single equation or when a particular interpretation is applied to one or the other. Similarly the equity yield and the bond rate are so closely related to each other that either would have the same effect in any specific model. Finally there is the implication that further analysis should center on periods longer than a single year.

Summary

The analysis of aggregate investment models proposed in prior studies with revised aggregate data for 1872-1914 has produced estimates which are consistent with those obtained by Neal for 1897-1914, but are inconsistent with the stage of growth hypotheses presented by Kmenta and Williamson.

However, the period separations used by Kmenta and Williamson have been supported. The division of the period from 1872 to 1914 into two sub-periods 1872-1895 and 1896-1914 significantly improved the results for every model tested.

The separation of total investment into two major components, track and equipment, did not improve the results to the extent which had been expected although several interesting patterns were observed. The models performed better for track than equipment in the early period while the reverse was true in the later period. In general all of the results for 1896-1914 were superior to those for 1872-1895, a pattern which was most apparent for models which included financial factors. None of the models explained equipment investment prior to 1895 well, but a distributed lag accelerator produced strong results for the period after 1896. The increasing importance of financial variables was clearly reflected in changing model structure between the two periods, a pattern which was most obvious in the equipment models.

While the aggregate results are suggestive they are not conclusive. The weak performance of the early period equipment models is particularly surprising. One would expect equipment investment to be more fully explained by a respons to the variables tested than track investment, which was probably based on longer term considerations. Similarly the impact of financial factors should impinge more clearly on track investment in the later period, since long term projects would be more sensitive to interest costs. But these specific puzzles are perhaps less important than the lurking suspicion that the periods of analysis are simply too short to permit strong conclusions from the observed variations in model performance. When those doubts are coupled with the strong suggestion of sharp regional variations in investment behavior and the consequent difficulty of relating macro coefficients to micro behavioral patterns, there is considerable cause for skepticism. One positive result of this exploration, however, is that it provides a consistent standard against which subsequent cross section and company time series results may be compared.

CHAPTER V

EMPIRICAL RESULTS: CROSS SECTION DATA

Introduction

The use of cross section data to analyze investment behavior is appealing for a variety of reasons. Perhaps the
overwhelming advantage of this approach is the dramatic increase in the number of degrees of freedom which can be made
available for statistical analysis compared to time series
data. This is particularly true in an analysis of investment behavior where the stability of the estimated relationship over extended periods of time is questionable. The use
of pure cross section data also reduces two of the principal
sources of error in the analysis of time series data, autocorrelation and multicollinearity. Finally several behavioral patterns such as age and size effects can be examined more directly in cross section data.

On the other hand it is clear that the results of cross
section analysis are not directly related to time series behavior. In particular there is a broad range of factors,
for example entrepreneurial talent, which vary among different firms at any point in time but which are relatively
constant for one firm over time. In his exhaustive study of
the relation of cross section and time series estimates

Edwin Kuh concluded that "these results indicate firm effects tend to nullify the desireable results of increasing size and/or averaging. Presuming 'errors will cancel out in the aggregate' for cross-sections can indeed be dangerously incorrect."[1]

In addition to the problem of accounting for the wide range of factors which may vary over the cross section, it is quite possible that variations in the size of companies in the sample could create a divergence from the assumptions of the regression model. It is likely that the variance of the error term will be related to the size of the sample company, violating the assumption of constant error variance. If this pattern is not corrected by a transformation of the variables or an elimination of extreme sizes in the sample, the least squares estimates will still be unbiased and consistent but an error arises in computing the standard error, and hence the significance, of the estimates.

The problems involved in the use of cross section data have been reduced in the following analysis by examining changes in consecutive cross sections over time, by including dummy variables for regional and system variations, and by testing for heteroscedasticity. An examination of the results for consecutive cross sections indicates the relative stability of different behavioral relationships, and

---

[1] Edwin Kuh, Capital Stock Growth, Op. Cit., p. 171.

isolates cyclical patterns which may affect time series specifications. The inclusion of dummy variables in the regression equations permits the data to be pooled to estimate parameters which are expected to be uniform over the sample more efficiently, and to be separated into more homogeneous groups for the estimation of other parameters which may vary over the sample. The use of dummy variables as well as the tests for autocorrelation and heteroscedasticity are discussed in detail below.

The remainder of this chapter presents the findings of the cross section regression analysis of investment behavior in the railroad sector from 1871 to 1914. The first section briefly discusses the properties of the sample and outlines the period divisions which were used in the analysis. The second section presents the models which emerged from a preliminary correlation analysis, and discusses some initial regression results for total investment. In the third section cyclical variations in the models are explored using investment data averaged over two year periods. Next, changes in investment behavior between the periods 1870-1895 and 1895-1914 are explored and the findings are related to the corresponding results from aggregate analysis in the last chapter. A final section provides a brief discussion of the tests for heteroscedasticity and autocorrelation.

The Sample

The sample consisted of nineteen railroad companies which reported annual data over the period from 1870-1914. The detailed properties of the sample, including a capsule history, are discussed in Appendix G. Annual observations on 25 variables were recorded for each company over the 45 year period, and annual data were averaged where necessary to reduce them to consistent June figures. Annual series of main track, other track, locomotives, passenger cars and freight cars were used to form annual series of gross investment in current dollars and gross capital adjusted for changing efficiency in 1910 dollars. Price data were insufficient to permit regional adjustments of the aggregate series, so the aggregate price indexes were used for companies as well. Although some bond rate and equity yield data were collected for various companies, the data were too limited to permit their inclusion in the cross section analysis.

In order to increase the available degrees of freedom for statistical analysis, the annual cross sections were combined to form moving sections over two or three year periods. In most cases the end years overlapped in consecutive cross sections. The period divisions for each moving section were derived from an analysis of the aggregate railroad investment cycles and were defined as follows:

(1) 1871-1873, (2) 1873-1875, (3) 1876-1878, (4) 1878-1880,
(5) 1880-1882, (6) 1883-1885, (7) 1885-1887, (8) 1888-1890,
(9) 1890-1892, (10) 1892-1894, (11) 1895-1897, (12) 1898-
1900, (13) 1900-1902, (14) 1903-1905, (15) 1905-1907,
(16) 1908-1910, (17) 1910-1912, (18) 1912-1914. These
divisions thus provide ten cross sections prior to 1895 and
eight cross sections after 1895 for an analysis of period
changes in investment behavior. Each cross section was
further classified as a period of expansion or recession
based on the aggregate railroad investment cycle. Nine of
the cross sections defined above - 1, 3, 4, 5, 7, 10, 12,
13, and 15 - were periods of expansion, while the remaining
nine were classified as periods of recession. These latter
classifications were used to study cyclical patterns in
investment behavior.

The use of pooled cross sections restores the possibility of autocorrelation in the regression analysis. The
sample data were arranged so that all observations for each
company were introduced consecutively, permitting the normal
test for autocorrelation through the Durbin-Watson statistic.
The moving sections were limited to two or three years in
homogeneous cyclical periods to minimize the impact of
excluded time variables on the sample estimates.

Companies were excluded from a cross section in years
for which they reported incomplete data, were operated by a

receiver, or underwent a merger or reorganization. This elimination had a significant impact on the sample size only in the period from 1895 to 1897, when the number of observations was reduced from 57 to 46.

Finally, regional and system dummy variables were defined for each company and included in all cross section regressions. The assumption was made that the coefficients of all the independent variables were the same in all regions and for all systems, but that the intercept term varied. This assumption may be illustrated using models for two regions which explain gross investment by lagged output alone:

$$I = a_1 + b X_{-1} \qquad \text{Region 1}$$
$$I = a_2 + b X_{-1} \qquad \text{Region 2.}$$

Separate regressions could be performed for each region but a more efficient estimate of b may be obtained by pooling data for both regions. This can be done by estimating the following equation:

$$I = a_1 Z_1 + a_2 Z_2 + b X_{-1} \qquad \text{Regions 1 and 2}$$

where Z_1 and Z_2 are regional dummy variables. Z_1 is defined as 1 if the company falls in region 1 and 0 if it does not, and similarly for Z_2 and region 2. This formulation is inconsistent with standard regression computer programs, but as J. Johnston observes this may be corrected by dropping one of the dummy variables.[2] Similarly the technique is easily extended to the use of dummy variables for different railroad systems which became increasingly important after 1895. The system and regional divisions used in the analysis are described in detail in Appendix G.

Models

The models of investment behavior used in the cross section analysis were designed to examine the changing importance of demand and supply factors. Because of the large number of regressions required to test each model over eighteen cross sections using total, track, and equipment investment as dependent variables, emphasis was initially placed on reducing the range of potentially relevant variables through correlation analysis. Three final equations were then explored in detail.

It was not possible to develop adequate data on bond rates, equity yields, and prices for individual firms over the entire period of analysis. Several alternate measures of the availability of funds were introduced in their stead including cash on hand, the ratio of debt to equity, interest payments, the annual surplus, retained earnings defined as net operating revenue minus dividends, and net operating revenue. Interest payments and net operating revenue had

---

[2] J. Johnston, Econometric Methods (New York: McGraw-Hill Book Co., 1963), p. 222.

the strongest simple correlation with annual investment. An
initial analysis of five regression models of total investment supported the selection of interest and net operating
revenue as the best representatives of the cluster of financial variables.

Similarly several stock adjustment and accelerator
models were explored. In contrast to the aggregate findings, the capacity pressure variable, defined as the minimum
prior ratio of gross capital to ton-miles of freight carried
multiplied by current ton-mileage, produced strong results.
The change in ton-mileage lagged one period consistently
produced the best accelerator results. On the other hand,
when lagged investment was introduced as an explanatory variable its coefficient was almost always insignificant and the
explanatory power of the other variables was reduced. Similarly a simple stock adjustment model including capital and
ton-mileage each lagged one period produced weak results.
In the latter formulation capital was significant in only
one of the eighteen cross sections and ton-mileage in only
three.

Table H1 presents the three models which were produced
by the preliminary explorations. Model 3-3 is based on demand factors including the change in ton-mileage as a measure
of accelerator influences and the capacity pressure variable.
In this case the inclusion of capital serves to measure the

impact of firm size and replacement demand on investment behavior. Model 3-6 contains net operating revenue and interest payments, the financial factors which initial analysis suggested were most relevant. The age of the firm was added to the model to explore the possible significance of life cycle factors. Capital again serves to measure firm size effects, particularly replacement demand, but could also have a retarding effect on investment in its stock adjustment role. Model 3-7 is identical to 3-6 except gross earnings are substituted for net earnings in an attempt to clarify the role of profits as a source of funds or a proxy for output.

In each model the two year average level of investment is used as the dependent variable. In effect this extends the lags on the independent variables to 1-1/2 years and takes cognizance of the interval between capital expenditures and actual additions. The use of lagged independent variables provides for a reasonable interval between the decision to invest and the actual addition of components to the capital stock. In addition the use of lagged data in a cross section analysis is highly desireable because in a pure cross section all lagged variables are both pre-determined and exogenous.[3] Although the lagged data are not

---

[3]Carl F. Christ, Econometric Models and Methods (New York: John Wiley and Sons, Inc., 1966), p. 235.

necessarily exogenous in pooled cross sections such as those used in this analysis, the risk of damaging simultaneous effects is reduced. For example it is quite possible that current investment could increase current revenue, and this simultaneous relationship could distort a single equation regression analysis of the hypothesis that revenue determines investment. But it is certainly unlikely that lagged revenues could be increased by current investment.

Cyclical Variations

Table H1 presents the results of ordinary least squares regressions using the eighteen overlapping cross sections with total, track, and equipment investment as the dependent variables. The cross section results are pooled for the periods 1871-1914, 1871-1895, 1895-1914, and periods of recession and expansion. In each case the coefficient listed represents a weighted average of the individual cross section coefficient estimates, where the weights are proportional to the reciprocal of the variance of each estimated coefficient. Thus those coefficients which are most significant are given the highest weight in the average. The figures in parentheses besides the coefficients represent the number of cross sections in which the coefficient was significant at the 98, 95, and 90 percent confidence levels respectively. By comparing these numbers with the number of cross sections in each period group, one obtains a

reasonable picture of the significance of the average coefficient. The R^2 listed is simply the mean of the squared
coefficients of multiple correlation, corrected for the
number of degrees of freedom, of the cross sections in the
group.

This section will examine only the results for the
periods of recession and expansion. Before examining the
coefficients of the models it may be helpful to examine the
mean R^2s alone in Table 5.1. Looking first at total and
track investment it is clear that cyclical effects had a
strong impact on the demand model (3-3) and a negligible
impact on the financial models (3-6 and 3-7). The R^2 of
the demand model jumped from .47 in the recession periods
to .56 in expansionary periods for total investment, and
from .42 to .52 for track investment. On the other hand
all three models reflected strong cyclical patterns for
investment in equipment with an increase in the R^2 from recession to expansion of +.17 for models 3-3 and 3-7 and
+.14 for model 3-6. All three models provide equivalent
results for equipment investment in both periods, but the
demand model works slightly better for track in the expansionary period, and the finance models, particularly 3-6,
have a higher R^2 in periods of recession. The two financial
models of track investment, on the other hand, produced
nearly identical results in both periods. One implication

Table 5.1

MEAN CROSS SECTION SQUARED CORRELATION COEFFICIENTS

Model	Period	Number of Cross Sections	R^2 by Component Total	Track	Equipment
3-3	1871-1914	18	.51	.47	.51
3-3	1871-1895	10	.52	.48	.56
3-3	1895-1914	8	.51	.46	.45
3-3	Recession	9	.47	.42	.42
3-3	Expansion	9	.56	.52	.59
3-6	1871-1914	18	.49	.48	.51
3-6	1871-1895	10	.46	.49	.55
3-6	1895-1914	8	.53	.48	.47
3-6	Recession	9	.48	.49	.45
3-6	Expansion	9	.50	.48	.59
3-7	1871-1914	18	.50	.47	.52
3-7	1871-1895	10	.46	.44	.55
3-7	1895-1914	8	.56	.50	.48
3-7	Recession	9	.49	.45	.43
3-7	Expansion	9	.52	.48	.60

Column	Description
Model	Model designations are explained in the notes to Table H1.
R^2	The R^2 listed is the average for all cross sections in the period group adjusted for the number of degrees of freedom.

of these results is that equipment investment is more re-
sponsive to changing demand and financial conditions in
periods of expansion than it is in periods of recession.
There is an even stronger indication that track investment
was tied to demand conditions in periods of expansion and
was more sensitive to financial constraints in recessionary
intervals.

An analysis of specific coefficients in Table H1 supports the pattern indicated by the model R^2s. In the demand
model (3-3) the coefficient of the change in ton mileage,
a_3, increases sharply between the recession and the expansion cross section groups for total, track, and equipment
investment. The increase in the coefficient of the capacity
pressure variable, a_2, is even more striking and there is a
substantial increase in its significance as well. The negative capacity pressure coefficient for equipment in recessionary periods is interesting, because it indicates a weak-
ening of the model when there is significant excess capacity.
The coefficients of capital are consistently positive, very
significant, and stable over the cycle, suggesting that the
capital variables in each model reflect replacement demand.

The interest payments coefficient is consistently negative in both portions of the cycle for models 3-6 and 3-7.
Although there is a slight suggestion of a more significant
retarding effect in the recessionary periods, in general the

coefficients and their significance are quite stable. On the other hand the age variable shows a strong cyclical pattern. In both models for track and equipment the age of the firm has a retarding effect in periods of expansion and a positive effect in periods of recession, although the number of significant coefficients was low. This result was most obvious in track investment where the age coefficients are significantly larger than those in the equipment models. In general net and gross earnings showed no cyclical patterns and there was little difference in significance between their respective coefficients. The capital coefficients increased between the recession and expansion phases for equipment but were roughly constant for track. Since most replacement of equipment was generally accomplished in periods of expansion this pattern supports the contention that the capital stock variable reflects demand for replacements.

It appears that the cyclical performance of the financial models in explaining investment in equipment largely rests on the changing significance of the capital coefficient. The interest and revenue variables show no strong cyclical patterns and the age effects are more evident in track investment. The sharp increase in replacement demand in expansionary periods thus explains the cyclical variations in the equipment financial models.

Age effects on track investment are interesting even though the age coefficients are not generally significant. The positive role of age in periods of recession is not surprising, because the older firms with established earnings records could easily have greater access to external funds in such periods. The retarding effect of age in periods of expansion is puzzling, but it is possible that the supply of external funds again provides an answer. If new firms can finance further extensions only when profits are high and money markets are more accessible, their investment is more likely to be concentrated in periods of expansion.

The cyclical performance of the demand model is the most striking, if not surprising, result of this analysis. The sharp increase in R^2 for both track and equipment in expansionary periods is reflected in substantial increases in the size and significance of the capacity pressure and accelerator variables. During periods of recession when there is excess capacity the coefficient of the capacity pressure term turns negative and the accelerator coefficient is much smaller. In such recessionary periods the financial models are more successful in explaining track investment.

Period Variations in Investment Patterns

In addition to the grouping of cross section results by homogeneous periods of the aggregate investment cycle, the results were compared using the time series period divisions

from the preceding chapter. Table H1 presents a summary of
the results for the periods 1871-1914, 1871-1895, and
1895-1914. A preliminary view of the results may be obtained by examining the pattern of the R^2s alone in Table
5.1.

Looking first at total investment the demand model (3-3)
shows little variation over the three periods, while the financial models (3-6 and 3-7) produce significantly higher
results after 1895. As a result the demand models produce
a slightly higher R^2 than the financial models in the early
period and a lower R^2 in the later period. This pattern
is also reflected in the track equations except that the
results for financial model 3-6 show no variation over the
two periods. All of the equipment models on the other hand
produced significantly higher R^2s in the period prior to
1895, a result which contrasts sharply with the aggregate
findings. Similarly all of the equipment models produced
better results than track for the period 1871-1895, and the
track models produced marginally better results than equipment for the period 1895-1914, a pattern which is precisely
the reverse of the aggregate conclusions.

These patterns were confirmed by an analysis of the coefficients of the different models shown in Table H1. In
model 3-3 there was a sharp decline in the size of the
accelerator coefficient and a less pronounced decline in its

significance between the periods 1871-1895 and 1895-1914.
Similarly the capacity pressure coefficient declined in
size and significance between the two periods for track and
total investment, although it was more stable for equipment.
The capital coefficient again remained positive, significant
and relatively constant over the two periods. Thus the
decline in the explanatory power of the demand model between the two periods may be attributed to the declining
significance of the capacity pressure and accelerator coefficients.

In the financial models (3-6 and 3-7) the interest coefficient showed a significant decline between the two
periods for total and track investment, while it remained
constant for equipment investment. Thus the retarding
effect of fixed interest payments on track investment was
substantially reduced after 1895. The impact of the age
variable was much less pronounced in the period analysis
than it had been in the cyclical explorations. Gross and
net earnings again had a consistent positive impact on investment, and while the significance of each earnings variable increased slightly in the later period this effect was
not pronounced. On the other hand the significance of the
capital stock coefficient was substantially lower in the
later period for equipment investment, although the size of
the coefficient changed very little. The decline in the

significance of the capital stock coefficient largely accounts for the decline in the R^2 of the financial equipment
equations. In the track models the drop in the significance
of capital was less severe and was balanced by a general improvement in the other variables, which produced a net increase in the R^2 between the two periods.

The analysis of coefficient structure thus indicates
that demand factors were more important in explaining equipment investment prior to 1895 than subsequently, but that
the response of track and total investment to such factors
did not change. The impact of financial factors may be
reduced to two central findings: (1) a reduction in the
retarding influence of fixed interest payments on track investment after 1895, (2) a substantial decline in the significance but not the size of the capital coefficient in
equipment investment models after 1895. The first result
is consistent with the easing of credit conditions after
1898 and the primary impact of the reduced cost of finance
on long term track investment. The increasing variance of
the estimated capital stock coefficient is more puzzling
since both the size and sign of the coefficient were the
same in both periods. If the capital stock variable is
interpreted as a measure of replacement demand, as its positive sign suggests, the implication is that while replacement remained a constant function of the capital stock for

the sample as a whole, it showed increased variance over individual companies in the later period. Since replacements are normally highest in expansion phases a possible explanation for this phenomenon is that investment cycles were less homogeneous over all regions after 1895. This divergence would decrease the homogeneity in response to cyclical factors in the cross sections, which were chosen by swings in aggregate investment, while the average response could well remain constant over time.

The period analysis thus produces several findings which diverge from the results of time series tests with aggregate data. First, all of the cross section models explained equipment investment more than track prior to 1895, and track more than equipment after 1895. This pattern was most striking in the early period. Second there is a decline in the explanatory power of the demand equations for equipment investment after 1895, while the aggregate results suggested that demand factors became increasingly important in equipment investment after 1895 but were not significant in the earlier period. Finally while the financial models improve sharply after 1895 this impact is limited to track, the clearest change being in the reduced retarding effect of interest payments. The aggregate results suggested that easing financial conditions had a sharper impact on equipment investment, but in the cross sections the financial models for equipment actually produced weaker results after 1895.

One further pattern emerged from an analysis of the individual results for each cross section. In all of the models tested the results for the periods 1871-1885, 1885-1892, 1898-1905, and 1908-1914 were generally internally homogeneous in terms of coefficient structure and model explanatory power. This was particularly true in the period from 1885-1892. These results are not surprising since the periods correspond to the cyclical pattern of aggregate investment, and earlier analysis suggested that cyclical variations were important in investment behavior. The implication of these findings is that four, rather than two, divisions in the time series analysis of the period from 1871-1914 might be required to accurately trace changes in investment behavior, but that if only two periods are to be examined a division around 1895 is acceptable.

Heteroscedasticity and Autocorrelation

Since moving cross sections were used in the preceding analysis, there is the possibility of autocorrelation of the error terms which could distort the statistical tests for the significance of the estimated coefficients. By placing all observations for each company in order in the cross section samples it was possible to use the normal Durbin-Watson test for autocorrelation. There was a suggestion of

autocorrelation in only five percent of the final equations
summarized in Table H1, and in no case was the Durbin-Watson
statistic less than 1.0.

The test for heteroscedasticity was less direct, however, and required a time consuming iterative procedure
which generally followed the development described by Edward
Kane in Economic Statistics and Econometrics.[4] The central
assumption of his technique is that the test variance is
equal to the true constant variance plus some size variable
raised to a constant power. Using the squared residual as
an estimate of the test variance of each observation, the
appropriate exponent for the size variable may be obtained
by regressing the natural logarithm of the test variance on
the natural logarithm of the size variable. The intercept
term in the estimated regression equation represents the true
constant variance and the coefficient of the size variable
is the desired exponent. If the coefficient of the size
variable is not significant the implication is that the variance is homoscedastic, as the regression model assumes, and
no transformation of the variables is required.

Table 5.2 reports the results of the tests for heteroscedasticity in models 3-3 and 3-6 for four selected cross
section periods. The gross capital stock was used as the

---

[4]Edward J. Kane, Economic Statistics and Econometrics
(New York: Harper and Row, 1968), p. 376.

size variable and the coefficient listed represents the
estimated capital exponent.

Table 5.2

TEST FOR HETEROSCEDASTICITY

| Model | Period | Capital Coefficient (t) | |
		Track	Equipment
3-3	1871-1874	.45 (1.4)	.44 (1.4)
	1890-1892	.54 (1.2)	1.07 (.2)
	1900-1902	.11 (.4)	1.94 (.4)
	1910-1912	.01 (.1)	.37 (.7)
3-6	1871-1874	1.34 (.4)	1.66 (.5)
	1890-1892	.54 (1.2)	1.07 (.3)
	1900-1902	.39 (1.0)	1.50 (.4)
	1910-1912	.03 (.2)	.09 (.2)

In no case was the coefficient of any track or equipment
model significant indicating that the test variance was uniformly homoscedastic. Thus no further transformations of
the variables were explored.

Summary

By examining the investment behavior of a sample of
nineteen companies in eighteen overlapping cross section
periods it was possible to reach several conclusions relating to the dynamic changes in investment behavior. The impacts of autocorrelation and heteroscedasticity were

negligible so that the added degrees of freedom from cross
section analysis could be fully exploited. The use of dummy
variables for system affiliations and regional divisions
provided a technique for pooling all of the observations to
produce efficient estimates of the model coefficients.

The preliminary analysis of simple correlation coefficients and a limited examination of total investment regression models isolated variables which appeared to play a
strong role in investment behavior. Three models were then
explored in detail to isolate the changing impacts of demand
and financial conditions over the cycle and between different periods. In each case the explanatory power of the
models as reflected in the R^2 was examined to provide an
initial indication of the important trends. The suggested
trends were then explored in detail by examining the changes
in estimated model coefficients.

The cyclical variations in the performance of the
models were striking. For all of the equipment models there
was the strong suggestion that replacement demand increased
significantly in periods of expansion. The demand model
showed a sharp improvement in explaining investment patterns
in expansionary periods, but produced weaker results in
recessionary periods of excess capacity. The financial
models for track remained remarkably stable over the cycle,
although there was a suggestion that younger firms invested

relatively more in expansionary periods than older firms,
and less in recessionary periods.

The summary results for the periods 1871-1895 and 1895-
1914 were most striking in their divergence from the implications of earlier aggregate analysis reported in Chapter
IV. The cross section implications, however, are all consistent with the qualitative record presented in Chapter II.
Prior to 1895 track investment is poorly explained by the
cross section models, but equipment investment was quite
sensitive to demand factors. The cross section results
also suggest that track investment after 1895 is best explained by financial factors, specifically the reduced retarding effect of interest payments. In contrast to the
aggregate results the impact of changed financial conditions
on equipment investment was not important.

These are not minor distinctions without a difference.
They suggest that component investment patterns diverged
significantly with equipment investment responding to demand
patterns and track extension after 1895 to financial conditions. Track extension prior to 1895, however, is poorly
explained although there are indications of rapid extensions
by new firms in periods of growing demand and eased financial constraints. But those track extensions are not explained by pressure on existing capital capacity. This
pattern is consistent with the qualitative record of

extension prior to 1895, which suggests that investment was
concentrated in periods of increased demand but was excessive relative to the requirements of current demand.

Finally there were implications as to the roles of
specific variables. No significant distinctions could be
found between gross and net operating revenues in any of the
models. In every case the capital coefficient was positive
and significant, showing strong cyclical patterns for equipment but little variation for track investment. This pattern strongly suggests that the capital stock variable
operated as a measure of replacement demand in the models
which were examined. The level of fixed interest payments
was generally the most significant financial variable, a
finding which is substantiated by the record of repeated
financial failures in the sector due to inordinate increases
in fixed interest charges. There was some evidence based on
the homogeneity of model structures that period divisions
of 1871-1895 and 1896-1914 for time series analysis are
consistent with the changes in cross section behavior.

CHAPTER VI

EMPIRICAL RESULTS: COMPANY TIME SERIES DATA

Introduction

In many ways all of the preceding discussion may be
viewed as background for the subsequent analysis of time
series investment behavior by nineteen sample companies over
the period from 1871 to 1914. This chapter is the heart of
the entire analysis of investment patterns in the railroad
sector since it focuses on the response of actual decision
making units to the central variables of investment theory.
While the cross section analysis was useful in examining cyclical variations and consecutive sections could be used to
draw conclusions on several interesting dynamic factors, the
time series data provide a vehicle for directly exploring
the impact of important financial variables, such as the
bond rate, and for examining regional variations in behavioral patterns. The overview in Chapter II of considerations
bearing on the investment decision suggested that regional
variations could be particularly important. Similarly the
change in investment behavior after the easing of credit conditions in 1898 can be examined in detail.

Two drawbacks of the time series analysis must again
be stressed. First, it is quite likely that investment

111

behavior cannot be explained by a stable array of factors
over long periods of time. The results of the cross section
analysis indicated that cyclical factors were particularly
important, and that homogeneous behavioral patterns could
be traced for periods no longer than ten to fifteen years.
Thus the difficulties of regression analysis over small
samples arise again. Second, the effects of multicollinearity
and autocorrelation may distort the usual tests for statistical significance. These problems can be limited, however,
by examining a number of decision making units and emphasizing the importance of homogeneity in the results for all
companies. Micro data are vastly superior to aggregate data
in terms of the multicollinearity problem because of the
increased variation of individual company series. Once
again autocorrelation problems can be detected and eliminated where necessary.

The outline of analysis in this chapter is quite similar to the pattern outlined in the study of cross section
results in Chapter V. First, the models used in the analysis are discussed and compared with aggregate and cross
section formulations. Second, the results for total, track,
and equipment investment for all companies are explored for
the periods 1871-1895 and 1896-1914. As with the cross section study, the R^2 pattern is first examined to isolate
potentially significant investment patterns and subsequent

discussion is directed at a detailed analysis of the model
coefficients. Comparisons of period and component results
for each company as well as summary results for all companies
are stressed. Next, regional patterns in the results are
explored to clarify the findings for all sample companies.
Finally, variations in investment in main and other track
are examined to elucidate the problems which were encountered
in explaining track investment prior to 1896. A summary
section briefly compares the company time series findings
with the results for cross section and aggregate data.

Models

The sample of nineteen companies used in the subsequent
analysis has been described in Chapter V and is explored in
some detail in Appendix G. Time series data on some twenty-
five variables were collected for each sample firm. Only
aggregate bond rates, equity yields, and price indexes were
available for the entire 44 years of this analysis, so those
aggregate series were used in the examination of company investment behavior. As in the cross section analysis, preliminary tests of annual total investment were conducted to
eliminate some of the potentially relevant variables and
focus subsequent detailed explorations on the most significant relationships.

The use of annual investment as the dependent variable
with independent variables lagged one period produced weak

results for four models of total investment which were ini-
tialy examined for the entire period 1871-1914. The coefficient structure of the Klein general model (1-1) used in
the aggregate analysis was good but the average r^2 of .26,
the highest of the preliminary models, was considered quite
low. Modifications of Neal's aggregate financial model
(1-2) showed that the addition of an accelerator variable
or the change in equity prices did not improve the results.
The coefficient structure of a simple stock adjustment using
lagged capital and ton-mileage was quite strong, and the
addition of lagged investment improved the results. On the
other hand the modified Eisner distributed lag model (1-3)
produced weak results, particularly in the sign structure
of the lagged accelerator terms.

Based on these preliminary results the dependent variable was changed to a two year average of investment, using
investment in the current and subsequent year. As for the
cross section analysis this change produces an increase in
the lag structure of all the independent variables to 1-1/2
years. Since the investment data are based on actual additions to the capital stock, the adjustment produces an investment variable which corresponds more closely to actual
current expenditures. The discussion in Appendix D suggests
that reported data on capital expenditures were most closely
related to actual capital additions in that same year, so an

added one-half year lag to account for the gap between expenditures and additions should be sufficient.

Table H2 presents the five models which emerged from
the preliminary analysis for further exploration. Model
2-1 is the Klein general model in the same form used in the
aggregate analysis. Model 2-2 is the Neal financial model
with the addition of a lagged price index, which the preliminary analysis suggested would improve the structure of
the model. Model 2-3 is identical to cross section model
3-3. Since the Eisner distributed lag model (1-3) produced
weak results in the initial tests, model 2-3 was substituted
to measure the impact of demand factors. The estimation
of the model in the same form as the cross section analysis
also permits a direct comparison of the cross section and
time series coefficients. Model 2-4 is a simple stock adjustment transformed into a distributed lag by the inclusion
of lagged investment as an independent variable. Model 2-5
is a revised version of Neal's financial model which cor-
rects for the criticism of Chapter III that the model should
include a measure of capital capacity. In this formulation
the capital stock is employed in lieu of an output variable,
change which has the added advantage that retained earnings and output, which have a high correlation with each
other, are not included in the same model as competing independent variables.

The first four models were explored in detail over the periods 1871-1895 and 1896-1914 using total, track, and equipment investment as dependent variables. Model 2-5 was then substituted for model 2-2 and the four models were examined using main and other track investment as dependent variables over the same period. In each case the capital and price variable used in the equation corresponded to the dependent variable. Thus four models were examined using five dependent variables over two time periods for nineteen separate companies. The results of those 760 regression equations are presented in summary form in Table H2 and are discussed in detail in the remainder of this chapter.

Total, Equipment, and Track Investment Results by Period

Table 6.1 summarizes the average R^2 for each model and capital component obtained from regression analysis of the nineteen sample companies over the periods 1871-1895 and 1896-1914. This section will focus on the results for models 2-1 through 2-4 using total, track and equipment investment as dependent variables. A subsequent section will examine model 2-5 and trace the patterns of investment in main and other track.

Two patterns in the averaged company R^2s are very similar to the results for aggregate data. First, the division of total investment into track and equipment investment does not significantly improve the results. The general effect

Table 6.1

MEAN COMPANY TIME SERIES SQUARED CORRELATION COEFFICIENTS

Model		Total	R^2 by Investment Component Equipment	Track Total	Main	Other
2-1	1871-1895	.38	.54	.35	.55	.61
2-1	1896-1914	.60	.61	.78	.66	.80
2-2	1871-1895	.45	.60	.40		
2-2	1896-1914	.63	.61	.56		
2-3	1871-1895	.42	.57	.33	.48	.56
2-3	1896-1914	.54	.59	.43	.50	.70
2-4	1871-1895	.46	.62	.41	.47	.70
2-4	1896-1914	.67	.64	.61	.56	.83
2-5	1871-1895				.47	.55
2-5	1896-1914				.50	.69

Column	Description
Model	Model designations are explained in Table H2.
R^2	The listed figure is the average R^2 for the nineteen sample companies corrected for the number of degrees of freedom.
Track	The estimates for main and other track were produced by models which employed three year averages of investment as dependent variables. The model for total track investment employed a two year average of investment as the dependent variable. As noted in the text direct comparison of the R^2s produced from these different models must be made with care.

to produce a higher R^2 for equipment than for total investment, and a lower R^2 for track. Only in the Klein general
model (2-1) in the period 1896-1914 are the R^2s of the track
and equipment models higher than the result for total investment. Second, the results for every model and component are
better for the period 1896-1914 than for 1871-1895. This
pattern is most striking in the track and total investment
models, the findings for equipment being far more stable.

On the other hand there are some clear divergences from
the aggregate pattern. All of the company models produced
results for equipment investment which were superior to the
corresponding model of track investment in every period,
with the single exception of the Klein model (2-1) in 1896-
1914. The aggregate results suggested that the track models
performed better than equipment models in the early period.
The company models produced particularly poor results for
track investment in the period 1871-1895, the R^2 of the four
track models falling an average of .20 below the comparable
equipment models.

The company results for track investment in 1896-1914
showed substantial improvement over the early period, the
average R^2 of .78 for the Klein model (2-1) being the most
impressive. There was much less variance in the equipment
results over the two periods and among the four models. The
stock adjustment model (2-4) produced the best results for

equipment investment in both periods, but the R^2 was only marginally higher than the other models and the inclusion of lagged investment in the model distorts such comparisons.

The analysis of the average R^2s for the nineteen company regressions of four models over different periods and components thus focuses attention on three patterns: (1) the poor performance of all the models in explaining track investment prior to 1896, (2) the sharp improvement in the track models after 1896, particularly in the Klein model (2-1), (3) the strong stable results for equipment investment in both periods. These patterns were explored and supported by a comparative analysis of the results for each company.

The equipment models produced higher R^2s than the corresponding track models for 90 percent of the companies in 1871-1895 and 77 percent of the companies in 1896-1914. This pattern is consistent with the noted poor performance of the track models in the early period, and the strong stable results for the equipment models. The R^2 for each company equipment model in 1896-1914 was higher than the result for 1871-1895 for only 56 percent of the companies, attesting to the stability of the equipment results. On the other hand the sharp increase in the results for track models in the later period was reflected by 64 percent of the companies. Thus the trends suggested by the average

R^2s for all companies are largely reflected throughout the sample.

Table H2 presents a summary of the coefficient estimates for each company time series model in the same format as the cross section table. The coefficient listed is a weighted average of the estimates for all nineteen companies, the weights being the reciprocals of the variance of each coefficient estimate. The numbers in parentheses to the right of each coefficient indicate the number of company regression equations in which the coefficient was significant at the 98, 95, and 90 percent confidence levels respectively, and the listed R^2 is the average for all of the sample companies. Each model will be examined in some detail.

Model 2-1. - - The most striking result for the Klein general model is the sharp increase in the size and significance of the bond rate coefficient in the track model after 1896. The track model has the correct a priori coefficient structure in both periods with the exception of a positive but insignificant bond rate coefficient in the early period. The improvement in the R^2 from .35 to .78 can be traced to the high significance of the bond rate in the later period, where the size of the coefficient increases dramatically and its sign becomes negative. The 1896-1914 equipment model produced results similar to the track model, except the bond rate coefficient was much smaller and less significant. The equipment model structure was poor in the early period. In short the model produced weak results in 1871-1895 for both track and equipment investment and its improved performance in the later period rested primarily on the strong impact of the bond rate, which was most evident in the track model.

Model 2-2. - - The Neal financial model modified with an added price index generally produced better results in 1896-1914 than the earlier period, although there were some problems with the model structure. The inclusion of ton-mileage and retained earnings in the same equation consistently produced a negative coefficient for retained earnings, suggesting that the two variables were too correlated to appear in the same model. In the 1871-1895 period the ton-mileage coefficient was negative for both the track and equipment models, but it turned positive after 1896. In the later period the coefficient of retained earnings, while still negative, became smaller and less significant. The equity yield apparently had a significant retarding effect in both periods, although the interpretation of the coefficient is questionable until the period after 1896 when the whole model structure is more acceptable.

Model 2-3. - - Tests of the capacity pressure and accelerator model for equipment investment produced strong results

in both periods. The capital coefficient was positive, significant, and stable over the two periods suggesting that
in this formulation capital serves as a measure of replacement demand. The capacity pressure coefficient was surprisingly negative and quite significant in the later period,
suggesting some excess capacity, although the coefficient
was very small. In both periods the accelerator coefficient
was positive and significant although it was larger and more
significant in the early period. The strength of the model
apparently rests on capital as a measure of replacement
demand and the positive impact of the accelerator term, and
both the equipment and track model structures are superior
in the early period despite their higher R^2s after 1896.
After 1896 the capacity pressure and accelerator terms are
negative and insignificant in the track model, while they
are positive and quite significant in the early period.
The role of the capital variable is very weak in the track
models, supporting the contention that it serves as a
measure of replacement demand in the equipment models. The
model thus produces good results for equipment investment in
both periods, although the accelerator pressures are strongest prior to 1896. The results for track after 1896 are
poor, but the accelerator and capacity pressure terms are
positive and significant in the early period.

Model 2-4. - - The track versions of the stock adjustment model produced weak results in both periods. Lagged investment dominated the capital and ton-mileage coefficients in the early period, and the positive capital coefficient in the later period makes interpretation of the model tenuous. The equipment models were superior in coefficient structure, the best results being obtained for 1896-1914. In that period the capital coefficient is strong and negative, the ton-mileage coefficient is small but positive and significant, and the lagged investment term is highly significant. The whole model is weaker in the early period, but the capital coefficient, while positive, is very small and the R^2 is quite high.

The detailed analysis of model coefficients thus largely supports the pattern suggested by the average R^2 discussion, although some new results are clear. First, there is a substantial improvement in the track models after 1896, which may be traced to the strengthened role of financial factors. In models 2-1 and 2-2 the bond and equity rates, as well as the entire coefficient structures, became much stronger in the later period. On the other hand the capacity accelerator and stock adjustment models produced weak results for track investment in both periods, either in model structure or R^2. Second, the demand oriented models produced strong results for equipment investment in both periods

with the capacity pressure and accelerator (2-3) marginally
better in the early period, and the stock adjustment version
(2-4) most acceptable after 1896. The impact of financial
factors was less pronounced in equipment purchases than in
track investment. Finally, none of the models produced
strong results for track investment in the early period.
The coefficients of the capacity accelerator (2-3) and the
Klein general model (2-1) were most consistent with the
a priori sign structures, but produced low average R^2s of
.39 and .35 respectively prior to 1896.

The findings that financial factors impacted primarily
on track after 1896, that demand models produced strong
results for equipment investment in both periods, and that
track investment prior to 1896 is poorly explained by the
models tested, are consistent with the implications of the
cross section analysis but diverge from the aggregate results. The aggregate study suggested that financial factors
impacted primarily on equipment after 1896 and that equipment investment was most poorly explained in the early period. This divergence is explored in detail in the remainder
of this chapter by examining regional investment patterns
and the distinctions between investment in main and other
track. Particular emphasis is placed on the puzzle of explaining track investment in the period prior to 1896.

Regional Investment Patterns

The individual company results which were summarized
over all regions in the preceding analysis will be examined
in this section based on the five regional divisions explained in Appendix G and illustrated in Figure G1. Essentially region 1 refers to New England, region 2 to the Middle Atlantic and Old Northwest, region 3 to the South,
region 4 to the Northwest and region 5 to the Southwest.
Regional averages of the company R^2 results are summarized
for models 2-1 through 2-4 in Table 6.2.

As in the analysis for all companies every equipment
model produced better results than the corresponding track
model in all regions prior to 1896. After 1896 the financial models (2-1 and 2-2) produced superior results for
track investment in regions 1 and 2, while in all other
regions and models the equipment R^2s remained higher than
track. This effect was so pronounced in model 2-1 that the
average R^2 for all companies is higher for track than equipment, the only model and period in which this was the case.
The R^2 of .95 for track model 2-1 in region 1, the Northeast, was particularly impressive considering the R^2 of .46
achieved by that model and region in the early period. In
model 2-2 the R^2 for region 2, the Middle Atlantic and Old
Northwest, increased from .27 in the early period to .65
after 1896. For model 2-1 that region showed an increase in

Table 6.2

REGIONAL AVERAGES OF COMPANY TIME SERIES

SQUARED CORRELATION COEFFICIENTS

Model	Period	Region	Equipment	Track
2-1	1871-1895	All	.54	.35
		1	.58	.46
		2	.44	.32
		3	.45	.23
		4-5	.69	.40
2-1	1896-1914	All	.61	.78
		1	.58	.95
		2	.40	.65
		3	.77	.54
		4	.69	.46
		5	.67	.55
2-2	1871-1895	All	.60	.40
		1	.59	.42
		2	.52	.27
		3	.55	.40
		4-5	.71	.53
2-2	1896-1914	All	.61	.56
		1	.49	.45
		2	.36	.65
		3	.77	.49
		4	.76	.59
		5	.75	.56
2-3	1871-1895	All	.57	.33
		1	.65	.45
		2	.49	.36
		3	.47	.28
		4-5	.69	.27
2-3	1896-1914	All	.59	.43
		1	.48	.27
		2	.48	.55
		3	.68	.49
		4	.68	.37
		5	.63	.38

Table 6.2 (Continued)

Model	Period	Region	Equipment	Track
2-4	1871-1895	All	.62	.41
		1	.66	.43
		2	.50	.46
		3	.53	.41
		4-5	.73	.42
2-4	1896-1914	All	.64	.61
		1	.45	.37
		2	.51	.64
		3	.60	.60
		4	.69	.64
		5	.69	.69

Column	Description
Model	Model designations are explained in the notes to Table H2.
Region	Regional divisions are discussed in Appendix G and portrayed in Figure G1. In general the divisions are as follows: Region 1 - New England; Region 2 - Middle Atlantic and Old Northwest; Region 3 - the South east of the Mississippi; Region 4 - Northwest; Region 5 - Southwest.

the R^2 from .32 to .65. Although most regions showed increases in almost every track model in the later period,
the sharp improvement in the financial models in the Northeast and Middle Atlantic regions was exceptional. In contrast those same financial models produced lower R^2s for
equipment investment after 1896 than they had in the early
period in regions 1 and 2.

In the early period track investment was poorly explained in every region and model, the highest R^2 being
.53. The poorest results were for the capacity accelerator
model in regions 3, 4, and 5 with average R^2s of .28 and
.27. Those regions also produced the poorest track results
in the stock adjustment model but the regional disparity is
less pronounced. Regional patterns are also less obvious
in the early period financial models of track investment,
although models 2-1 and 2-2 produced weaker results in
regions 2 and 3, the areas which accounted for most track
construction in that interval.

A regional analysis of track investment thus suggests
that the impact of financial factors after 1896, which was
observed in the earlier analysis of all companies, was most
important in regions 1 and 2, New England and the Middle
Atlantic and Old Northwest. The weak performance of the
track models in the early period is quite homogeneous over
all regions, but is most apparent in the demand oriented

formulations (2-3 and 2-4) for the South, Southwest, and Northwest. Financial constraints may have been less important in the South and the Middle Atlantic and Old Northwest areas prior to 1896 than they were in New England and the Northwest and Southwest, although the disparity was not as great.

In contrast to the track analysis equipment investment is well explained by demand models in all regions in both periods. In general the results for regions 3, 4, and 5 were somewhat higher than for Eastern regions 1 and 2 in both periods. The financial models (2-1 and 2-2) were far more stable for equipment than for track investment over the two periods of analysis, with the R^2s rising slightly in regions 3, 4, and 5, and surprisingly falling in regions 1 and 2. Thus the equipment models suggest a pattern of stable regional response to financial and demand conditions with the demand equations producing marginally superior results in both periods.

But as prior analysis has repeatedly demonstrated the R^2 tells only a limited part of the story. Table H3 presents summary regional coefficients of track and equipment models 2-1 and 2-3. Once again the coefficient is a weighted average of individual time series coefficients and the numbers in parentheses are the number of regressions in which the coefficient was significant at the 98, 95, and 90

percent confidence levels respectively. The subsequent
analysis of coefficient structure will examine the four
central implications of the R^2 analysis: (1) the sharp improvement of the financial models (2-1 and 2-2) after 1896
was most apparent for track investment in regions 1 and 2,
(2) the demand models (2-3 and 2-4) produced the weakest
results for track investment prior to 1896 in regions 3,
4 and 5, (3) the financial track models prior to 1896 were
generally weaker in regions 2 and 3, (4) the equipment demand models consistently produced strong results in all
regions in both periods, while the equipment financial
models were generally much weaker.

Looking first at the regional results for model 2-1
in Table H3 from 1871-1895, it is clear that the impact of
the bond rate on track investment was quite weak. In contrast the results for 1896-1914 indicate a sharp increase
in the significance and size of the coefficient in all
areas but region 5, the Southwest. The structure of the
Klein model is strong in regions 1, 2, and 3 in the latter
period, although the sign of the capital coefficient is
positive in region 1. Region 4 has a much weaker bond rate
coefficient and a negative profits coefficient. The analysis of model structure thus underscores the R^2 finding that
the improvement in the financial track models after 1896 was
centered in regions 1 and 2, but there are indications of a

strong impact of financial factors in the South as well.
The increased significance of the interest rate accounts for
most of the improvement in the model.

The regional structure of track model 2-3 in 1871-1895
suggests that investment in regions 1 and 2 was responding
to strong accelerator pressures, but no capacity pressure or
accelerator coefficients were significant in regions 3, 4,
or 5. This observation supports the R^2 indication that
track demand models prior to 1896 produced the poorest results in the South, Southwest, and Northwest. On the other
hand the track model 2-1 is apparently weakest in regions
2 and 3 prior to 1896, regions 4 and 5 producing the only
correct model structure. No bond rate coefficients were
significant in regions 2 and 3, the areas containing most
track extension in that period. The performance of the
model in region 1 rested primarily on the strength of the
profit coefficient.

The analysis of track models 2-1 and 2-3 prior to 1896
thus presents an interesting picture of track expansion.
In region 1 the reaction to demand pressures was moderate
and investment showed a strong response to profits, while
in region 2 demand pressures were very strong and there was
little response to financial factors. Regions 4 and 5
showed no significant response to demand factors but track
investment was apparently sensitive to the cost of finance.
Neither model produced strong results in region 3.

The picture presented by the equipment models, as suggested by the R^2 pattern, diverges sharply from the track results. Model 2-3 produced strong results in every region prior to 1896, the capital and accelerator coefficients being particularly significant. Once again the capital coefficient was positive, stable, and significant in every region, suggesting that the capital variable serves as a measure of replacement demand in this formulation. The equipment accelerator term is strong in every region in the early period, particularly in New England, and every capacity pressure coefficient is positive. The results after 1896 are more mixed but demand pressures were still important in regions 3, 4, and 5. In region 1 the capital coefficient increased in size and significance, suggesting strong replacement demand, but the capacity pressure and accelerator terms turned negative. Only the accelerator term remained positive in region 2.

Equipment model 2-1, on the other hand, produced much poorer results. Although the bond rate coefficient was negative in every region prior to 1896, none of the coefficients was highly significant. The model structure is only correct in regions 4 and 5, the profits coefficient being negative in every other region. After 1896 the results are no more impressive with the single exception of region 3. The whole model structure is strong in the South and every coefficient is highly significant. In contrast regions 1, 2 and 5 have negative profits coefficients and region 4 has a positive bond rate coefficient, although the coefficients are largely insignificant.

This examination of the model coefficient structures in different periods confirms the implications of the R^2 analysis. The sharp improvement in the financial models after 1896 is centered in regions 1 and 2, although there was a strong response to such factors in the South as well. The equipment models showed very little response to the eased financial conditions. The investment pattern prior to 1896 suggests that while none of the models is particularly successful in explaining track investment in any region, the demand models are much weaker in the South, Southwest and Northwest, and the financial models produced the poorest results in regions 2 and 3. On the other hand the equipment demand models produced strong results in all regions prior to 1896 and in the South, Southwest and Northwest after 1896. Replacement demand apparently played a strong role in equipment investment in the Northeast after 1896, but the models produced poor results for equipment investment in region 2.

Investment in Main and Other Track

Although the regional analysis in the preceding section clarified many of the trends observed in the company time series data, one major puzzle remains. Track investment prior to 1895 was poorly explained by the models tested, particularly in the South, Southwest, and Northwest, but the results for equipment investment in those same areas were quite strong. The conflicting results for track and equipment suggest that the two year average level of investment used as the dependent variable is too short a period of analysis for track investment. Further, the regional disparities indicate that the poorest results are obtained in regions of main track extension, and that separate analysis of investment in main and other track might clarify the importance of such distinctions.

The subsequent discussion explores the results of regression analysis based on three year averages of investment in main and other track. Two year averages of all the independent variables were used to maintain the same lag structures in the models. The Neal financial model (2-2), which obtained relatively poor structural results in the analysis of track and equipment investment, was modified by replacing the ton-mileage variable with gross capital, as discussed above, and relabeled as model 2-5. The price index was omitted in the new model because of the extended time period and the use of average data. The detailed coefficient estimates for models 2-1, 2-3, 2-4, and 2-5 for main and other track investment are presented in summary form for 1871-1895 and 1896-1914 in Table H2.

Once again the initial analysis will be focused on the R^2 pattern in Table 6.1. Unfortunately autocorrelation problems, which were uniformly insignificant in the analysis of two year average investment in track and equipment, became quite significant in the three year average models of main and other track investment, which employed averaged independent variables. Thus the results for main and other track may be compared with each other, but comparison with the other models is not appropriate.

Several striking patterns are suggested by the R^2 results. Every model of other track investment obtained results which were superior to the corresponding main track model. The main track results were weakest in the early period, but the disparity with the findings after 1896 was much less than the examination of total track investment had suggested. On the other hand, the results for other track investment showed a marked improvement after 1896 with an average increase in the R^2 of .15, compared to an average increase in main track models of .08. The stock adjustment model (2-4) produced the best results for other track investment in both periods, although the inclusion of lagged investment in the model accounts for part of this disparity and the Klein general model (2-1) also produced strong results after 1896. In contrast the Klein model (2-1) produced the best results for main track investment

in both periods by some margin, and showed the sharpest increase of any main track model after 1896.

According to the R^2 pattern investment in other track
behaved very much like equipment, although there was a clear
response to financial factors in the other track models
after 1896 which was not observed for equipment. The results for main track investment are quite similar to the
findings for aggregate track investment in Chapter 4 with a
generally poor performance by all but the Klein model prior
to 1896, and a significant improvement in all models after
1896 with the best results again obtained by the Klein
model.

But an analysis of the model coefficient structures in
Table H2 requires several important modifications to these
conclusions. The Klein main track model (2-1) consistently
produces a positive coefficient for the bond rate although
it is small and insignificant in the early period, and after
1896 there is a strong negative coefficient for the profit
variable. Thus the model operates largely as a stock adjustment in the early period and breaks down after 1896.
In contrast the Klein other track models have a strong coefficient structure in both periods except for a positive
capital coefficient prior to 1896. The profits coefficient
became less significant in the later period but the interest
rate coefficient increased sharply in size and significance.

Thus there is a strong suggestion that financial conditions had a sharper impact on investment in other track than they did on main track extension, particularly after 1896.

Demand model 2-3 produced strong coefficients for both main and other track prior to 1896, but the accelerator term was far more significant for other track investment. After 1896 the other track model weakened substantially and its capacity pressure coefficient turned negative, while main track showed a stronger response to the accelerator. In the later period the stock adjustment model produced strong results for other track investment and there was a sharp increase in the coefficient of lagged investment, suggesting a faster reaction to increases in output. This pattern is consistent with the sharp increase in the output coefficient, although the positive capital coefficient in the early period weakens the interpretation of that model. The main track stock adjustment model coefficients were far less signifi-cant in both periods and the increase in the coefficient of lagged investment in the later period was much smaller. The results of model 2-5 were generally poor for both main and other track.

The coefficient structure thus suggests that while accelerator and stock adjustment pressures were significant in other track investment in both periods, the eased finan-cial conditions after 1896 also had a major impact on other

track investment, as shown by the increased significance of
the bond rate and the more rapid adjustment of capital to
the desired level. On the other hand financial conditions
had a limited impact on main track investment, which was
poorly explained in both periods but showed an increased reaction to demand conditions after 1896.

The examination of three year average investment in
main and other track thus accounts for much of the regional
variation in investment patterns. In New England, the Middle Atlantic and Old Northwest, and the South track investment after 1896 was primarily composed of intensive additions
to other track. Those regions showed the sharpest reaction
to financial conditions in the later period since other
track investment was sensitive to financial changes. In the
Southwest and Northwest where main track extension remained
the principal component of track investment through 1914,
the track models showed much less reaction to financial
conditions. After 1896 there are signs of an increased
sensitivity of main track investment to demand conditions,
but prior to 1896 main track extension is still largely
unexplained by the models tested. This latter finding is
consistent with the qualitative evidence presented in
Chapter II, a concomitance which will be explored at length
in Chapter VII.

Summary

It is clear that disparities in investment behavior for
different capital components were important in the period
from 1870 to 1914 and accounted for much of the observed
regional variation in investment behavior. The analysis of
the company time series examined this relationship in three
stages. After an initial exploration of total investment
to isolate the strongest relevant variables, four models
were examined using total, track and equipment investment
as dependent variables over the periods 1871-1895 and 1896-
1914. Regional patterns in those regressions were then explored to trace the impact of financial factors after 1896
and the poor explanation of track investment prior to 1896.
Finally the divergences in the models for main and other
track investment averaged over three year periods were examined to elucidate the observed regional disparities.

The investment patterns which have been gleaned so
laboriously from model coefficient structures and tests for
significance may now be expounded quite succinctly. Investment in rolling stock was best explained in both periods of
analysis by models containing accelerator and stock adjustment mechanisms, and there was little regional or period
variation in the results. Track investment responded significantly to eased financial conditions after 1896, a pattern which was most apparent on roads east of the Mississippi.

This trend is largely explained by the concentration of
other track investment in the East and the clear response
of other track investment to financial conditions. Main
track extensions, on the other hand, were poorly explained
by any of the models, although there were signs of increased response to demand factors after 1896. Thus the
models produced uniformly poor results in the early period
for total track investment which was then largely composed
of main track extensions, and the worst results were obtained in the West and South where most extensions were
concentrated. The use of three year average investment did
not appreciably improve the results for main track extension.

This sketch is quite consistent with the implications
of the cross section results. Prior to 1895 track investment was poorly explained by the cross section models, but
equipment investment was sensitive to demand conditions.
Similarly the cross section results suggested that track
investment after 1895 was best explained by the reduced retarding effect of fixed interest payments, while equipment
investment had a stable relationship with variations in
demand.

On the other hand both the cross section and company
time series findings diverge from the implications of the
aggregate time series study. The aggregate analysis produced the weakest results for equipment investment prior to

1895 and suggested that eased financial conditions after
1896 impacted primarily on equipment investment. Although
nearly every aggregate track model tested showed a sharp
improvement after 1896, it was not possible to show clear
distinctions among the results for different models.

Two central conclusions of the company time series
analysis must be stressed. First, the finding that main
track extension prior to 1896 was poorly explained by the
models tested is supported by the homogeneity of the results
regardless of model specification or the use of annual or
two or three year average investment data. Considerable
emphasis was placed on improving the early period results
for the track models without success. Second, the impact
of eased financial conditions after 1896 was evident throughout the analysis. It was perhaps most obvious in the role
of the bond rate in track, specifically other track, investment where the change in the size, significance, and in some
cases the sign of the coefficient was striking. But the
effects of easing financial constraints were also observed
in the coefficients reflecting the speed of adjustment of
the capital stock to the desired level.

CHAPTER VII

CONCLUSIONS

Introduction

At this juncture the results of roughly fourteen hundred regression equations have been reported in some detail, and a respite from the examination of tests for significance is certainly welcome. The decision to examine investment in different capital components dramatically increased the number of regressions required to test even the small number of models used in the analysis, and the need to summarize the results by regional groupings further complicated the presentation. Both component and regional distinctions, however, proved to be particularly important and the added complexity of the analysis was justified by the increased clarity of the results.

Time series analysis of investment behavior by nineteen sample firms over the period from 1871 to 1914 formed the backbone of the study, and some 950 regression equations were examined to trace distinctions for different components and periods. Much of the subsequent synthesis of the qualitative and quantitative findings will relate to the patterns observed in that company time series analysis. The cross section results largely related to cyclical variations, the importance of specific variables, and a limited number of observed dynamic patterns in changing model structures. Thus the cross section analysis was used primarily to gain insight into the appropriate specification of the company time series models and to indicate possible problems in the time series analysis. To a lesser degree the cross section findings serve as an independent check on the time series results.

An examination of aggregate investment models proposed in former studies was conducted to test for the sensitivity of prior estimates to the use of revised aggregate data, and to provide a standard against which company time series and cross section results could be compared. The findings of Kmenta and Williamson[1] were very sensitive to the aggregate data used in their analysis, while there was substantial support for the data and estimates produced by Neal.[2] On the other hand major disparities between the aggregate and company results suggested that regional and component distinctions made the analysis of investment behavior with aggregate data in this period inappropriate.

_____

[1]Jan Kmenta and Jeffrey Williamson, "Determinants of Investment Behavior: United States Railroads, 1872-1941," Op. Cit.

[2]Larry Neal, "Investment Behavior by American Railroads, 1897-1914," Op. Cit.

The remainder of this chapter explores the patterns of investment behavior suggested by the aggregate, cross section, and company time series results and relates them to the available qualitative evidence on investment behavior in the period 1870-1914. The headings for the remaining sections trace the exposition of specific conclusions relating to: (1) data, (2) comparison of cross section and time series methods, (3) comparison of aggregate, cross section and company time series regression results, (4) synthesis of the qualitative and statistical records, (5) the life cycle hypothesis, (6) methodology, (7) areas for further study.

Data

A principal contribution of this study is the development of a consistent set of annual aggregate investment, capital, output, earnings, employment, price, and capital component efficiency series for the railroad sector over the period from 1870 to 1914. In Appendixes A through E great care has been taken to explain the derivation of each series and to compare the series with alternate estimates wherever possible. Most of the series are presented in Table F1 which contains the data employed in the aggregate regression analysis. Separate company capital, investment, output, and earnings series were also compiled for the nineteen sample firms over the period 1870-1914, and while space prevents the reproduction of those series in this paper the data are available on computer print-outs and punched hollerith cards.

Although detailed comparisons of the aggregate data with alternate estimates are provided in the appendixes, the results for capital and investment should be stressed. The close agreement of the gross investment series in current dollars with Neal's estimates for 1896-1914, as shown in Figure D1, is striking. Separate estimates suggested that my gross investment series accounted for roughly 75 percent of total investment in this period, and that is precisely the observed divergence from Neal's results. In contrast there was substantial disagreement of my gross investment figures with those produced by Ulmer[3] for the entire period 1872-1914, as shown in Figure D2. In particular the disparity prior to 1890 suggests that Ulmer's investment series underestimates the actual flow of capital expenditures by some margin.

Similar comparisons of the capital series are not possible, since no other estimates attempt to measure capital by its capacity rather than its cost. The touchstone of capital aggregation was the relative contribution of each component to current production rather than the hypothetical cost of reproducing each component in some base year.

---

[3]Melville Ulmer, Capital in Transportation, Op. Cit.

Efficiency adjustments were based on the physical properties
of each capital component vintage, and depreciation schemes
based on changes in component prices with age were avoided
because of the tenuous relationship of changes in prices
with changes in efficiency. The gross capital stock composed of physical series adjusted for changing efficiency
over time corresponds most closely to the capital stock
variable discussed in investment theory.

Comparison of Cross Section and Time Series Methods

The agreement of the principal conclusions on investment behavior derived from the cross section and company
time series results has already been stressed and will be
reviewed in the following section. Because of the composition of the sample the time series results could be used
more effectively to analyze regional distinctions, but the
cross section analysis provided important indications of
cyclical as well as period variations. Only one of the
models was used in the same form in both the cross section
and time series regressions, because of the importance of
time variables in observed investment patterns. However
the coefficient estimates for the capacity and accelerator
models (2-3 and 3-3) are quite comparable and the results
provide an important insight into the general comparison
of time series and cross section data.

Both the cross section and company time series equipment models (2-3 and 3-3) produced almost identical results for both periods of analysis. That is, the summary time series equations based on the results for all nineteen companies were very similar to the corresponding results for all ten cross sections prior to 1895 and all eight cross sections after 1895. Consider for example the time series equipment results for 1871-1896 in Table H2, and the cross section equipment results for 1871-1895 in Table H1, for models 2-3 and 3-3 respectively:

Table 7.1

COMPARISON OF CROSS SECTION AND TIME SERIES
COEFFICIENTS AND R^2

	a_1	a_2	a_3	R^2
Cross Section	+.0411(7,7,9)	+.0001(2,3,4)	+.0176(6,7,8)	.51
Time Series	+.0478(8,10,11)	+.0002(1,1,2)	+.0183(9,10,13)	.54

Once again the coefficients a_1, a_2, and a_3 are weighted averages for all the regressions, the parentheses contain the number of coefficients significant at the 98, 95 and 90 percent confidence levels, and the R^2 is the average for all regressions. The correspondence of coefficients a_1 and a_3

and the R^2 is also striking in the models for the later period, and although the sign on a_2 differs in those equations the significance of the coefficients are low.

In contrast there are sharp disparities in similar track equations with considerable divergence in the size and signs of the coefficients in both periods, and in the overall R^2 for the models prior to 1895. These different results for cross section and time series comparisons reflect the underlying regional heterogeneity of track and the homogeneity of equipment investment behavior. Apparently the assumption that the structural coefficients were the same in all regions, which was used to defend the use of dummy variables for the constant term alone, in the cross section analysis was not justified. In the equipment equations, however, investment behavior was far more stable over all regions and the results of the cross section and time series regressions were more comparable.

Thus the evidence presented here carries the strong suggestion that homogeneous cross sections may provide consistent indications of time series behavior. On the other hand where major disparities in the behavior of individual companies based on regional or other distinctions which cannot be incorporated in the cross section model exist, cross section estimates are likely to be a poor guide to time series behavior.

Comparison of Aggregate, Cross Section, and Company Time Series Regression Results

Most of the specific findings of the three methods of analysis have already been related in separate summary sections, and were compared in the conclusion to the company time series analysis in Chapter VI. The most striking aspect of that comparison was the close agreement of the cross section and company time series results and the major disparities of those results with the aggregate findings.

The pattern which emerged from the company time series and cross section analysis demonstrated the importance of regional and capital component distinctions. Equipment investment in 1871-1895 and 1896-1914 was best explained by accelerator and stock adjustment mechanisms with considerable cyclical fluctuation due to the lumping of retirements in periods of expansion. Cyclical effects were also important in the demand models for track investment which had sharp increases in significance in expansionary periods, while the relationship with financial factors was more stable. Period distinctions were important in the track models which consistently obtained poor results prior to 1896 but improved significantly thereafter, particularly in models containing the bond rate or equity yield. This pattern was reflected in the cross section analysis by the reduced retarding effect of fixed interest payments, and in the time series results by the coefficients and significance of measures of financing costs. The observed concentration of the financial impact on track investment in the East led to a detailed analysis of investment in main and other track, which indicated that the financial impact after 1896 was most important on investment in other track. Other track investment in the early period was best explained in both periods compared to the results for other components. There were some indications of an increased reaction of main track extension to demand factors after 1896, but in the early period such investment was largely unexplained by the models tested.

In contrast, the aggregate results indicated that track investment was reasonably well explained by the Klein general model (1-1) prior to 1896, but poor results were obtained for all equipment models in that early period. The aggregate results also suggested that the impact of changed financial conditions after 1896 was most evident in the equipment models. While aggregate financial models of track investment after 1896 also produced good results, alternate demand models were almost as strong making interpretation of the results difficult.

The major distinction of the company and aggregate results, therefore, is the component which is singled out as the vehicle of changing investment behavior between 1872-1895 and 1896-1914. Both analyses suggest that all models improved in the later period and that financial factors became more important. But the aggregate findings suggest a major change in equipment investment with a more stable, albeit increasingly significant, pattern of track investment. The company results imply that equipment investment had a stable response to demand conditions in both periods and that financial changes produced new behavioral patterns of track investment after 1896. The aggregate results thus direct attention to equipment investment, while the company findings point to the central role of changing track investment patterns.

Synthesis of the Qualitative and Statistical Records

The major contention of this section is that the investment pattern suggested by the company time series and cross section results is consistent with the available qualitative evidence in the period from 1870 to 1914, while the aggregate findings are at variance with that qualitative record. The analysis of the major trends which impacted on investment behavior in Chapter II suggested that two factors were of dominant importance in investment behavior from 1870 to 1914: (1) the extension of main track into new regions of the South and West, principally motivated by long term expectations or construction profits, (2) the reorganization of money markets after 1898 and the emergence of financial institutions with strong continuing ties to the railroad sector, intermediaries which were capable of tapping the expanded capital markets. Each of these conclusions will be compared with the statistical record.

First, I find little advantage in addressing the question of whether or not the railroads built "ahead of" or "behind" demand in the period from 1871 to 1895. There are clear suggestions that main track extensions proceeded most rapidly in periods of increased demand, primarily in response to improved grain prices. Grain prices in turn responded to the restoration of Southern markets after the Civil War and to subsequent changes in international demand. But for a variety of reasons the response to each stimulus was excessive in terms of the requirements of current demand, a fact which may easily be documented in the record of receiverships, poor dividend payments, the discontinuities of extensive construction, the construction of parallel lines for extortion schemes, and less directly in excesses of construction charges. It hardly seems plausible that in the face of repeated cyclical disasters entrepreneus would view any current increases in demand as permanent and adjust their main track mileage accordingly. But it is quite likely that in such periods of expansion financial capital became more plentiful, and therefore track extensions which bore only the promise of future traffic and land returns could be undertaken. On the other hand the addition of other track and equipment could be expected to yield prompt returns in periods of expansion and was more sensitive to actual changes in road traffic.

Thus the company time series finding that main track extension was poorly explained by models containing only current demand factors prior to 1896, and that this pattern was most evident on Southern and Western roads where main track extension was concentrated, is quite consistent with the qualitative record. Further the cross section findings confirmed the cyclical instability of the response of track investment to demand factors and suggested that younger companies, largely located in the South and West, tended to invest relatively more in periods of expansion when external financing was more available. On the other hand investment in equipment and other track showed a clear response to demand conditions, and the observed cyclical instability of equipment investment was traced to the policy of concentrating replacements in periods of expansion. The company findings thus confirm the three major suggestions of the qualitative evidence: (1) main track extension was based on long term considerations which are not measured by the models tested and which may well defy quantification, (2) main track extensions tended to proceed cyclically in response to eased financial conditions, (3) equipment and other

track investment was largely based on response to the requirements of current demand.

The recovery from the crisis in 1893 produced three
trends which made future railroad investment more sensitive
to financial conditions. First the pattern of reorganizations generally produced a level of fixed interest charges
roughly equal to expected annual net earnings, and depressed
equity prices on the reorganized roads. Hence further expansion on those roads, largely reorganized by new banking
interests, rested on a recovery of equity markets or eased
bond rates. Second the banks retained control of the reorganized roads to protect their investments and insure
cooperation among roads in which they had an interest.
These institutions provided new financial intermediaries
through which the railroads could tap reorganized money and
capital markets. Finally, the pattern of mergers, where
controlling equity in the merged company was purchased by
the parent through the issue of collateral trust bonds, increased the impact of financial conditions on railroad investment.

The company time series and cross section results indicate that after 1896 changes in the cost of investable
funds impacted most sharply on track investment on roads
east of the Mississippi, particularly on investment in other
track. Although there were also increases in the response

of equipment investment to such factors, they were much less pronounced and demand factors continued to explain expenditures on rolling stock most satisfactorily. These effects were observed in the size and significance of the bond rate coefficient in the time series models, the interest payment coefficient in the cross section analysis, and indirectly in the rate of adjustment in the stock adjustment time series models. No models worked particularly well for main track, but there were indications of increased response to demand factors after 1896.

It is clear that there were divergent behavioral patterns for investment in main track, other track, and rolling stock, but it is not obvious why financial conditions should impact most sharply on other track investment. One distinction with rolling stock investment, which may have been important, was the existence of secondary markets for used equipment and the widespread use of equipment leases. Thus the rolling stock investment was not as fixed as track construction and the time horizon for such investment could be much shorter. As a result the impact of financial costs could well be very small on equipment investment, despite the comparatively long average life of rolling stock. The differences of main and other track investment after 1896 are less apparent, but it is possible that main track extension was based more on system competition and the desire to maintain a high market share than other track investment, which responded to more marginal demand and supply of funds considerations.

At any rate the composition of track investment had a marked impact on its response to changing market conditions. The poor performance of the track equations prior to 1896 may be traced to those regions which contributed the largest share of main track extensions, the South and West. After 1896 the improved performance of the track equations, and particularly for financial models, was centered in the roads east of the Mississippi which had the highest percentage of other track investment.

The company time series and cross section results are thus quite consistent with the qualitative pattern of main track extension prior to 1896 in response to long term considerations, the strong impact of financial conditions on track investment after 1896, and the consistent response of equipment investment to demand conditions. On the other hand the aggregate results diverge from each of these patterns, suggesting that track extensions prior to 1896 were more fully explained than equipment investment, and that the impact of eased financial conditions was principally on equipment investment.

Thus it appears that regional disparities in investment behavior were particularly important in the period from 1870

to 1914, and that the use of aggregate data to examine investment patterns in this interval can easily lead to faulty
conclusions. On the other hand both company time series and
cross section analysis produced similar insights into investment behavior which were largely consistent with independent qualitative evidence. In addition the use of company data increased the number of observations for statistical analysis to the point where considerable confidence may
be placed in the results.

The Life Cycle Hypothesis

The suggestion that changes in investment behavior in
the railroad sector from 1870 to 1914 corresponded to changes
in the age of the sector in some determinant manner is particularly misleading and may easily direct attention to
unimportant relationships. The sole distinction between the
periods 1870-1895 and 1896-1914 suggested by the Kmenta and
Williamson formulation of the hypothesis was the increased
restriction on the entry of new firms in the latter period,
and hence a reduced importance of profit rates in total investment. Their concentration on the changing age of the
sector allowed them to overlook the most important change in
investment behavior after 1896, the reorganization of money
markets and the increased importance of financial conditions
in the investment decision.

Further, the regional heterogeneity of railroad investment prior to 1914 makes the formulation of an aggregate
model of changing investment patterns in that period quite
misleading. The regression analysis of such an aggregate
function assumes a normal distribution of responses by each
firm around some representative relationship. For example,
the Kmenta and Williamson model for 1872-1895 contains a
stock adjustment mechanism based on the assumption that increases in output are viewed as permanent and the stock of
capital is accordingly expanded. But what interpretation
can be placed on this model if Eastern roads experienced the
increase in output and Western roads expanded based on long
term expectations? Similarly if, as Kmenta and Williamson
suggest, profit conditions were the primary stimulus to new
firm entry prior to 1896, what interpretation can be placed
on the simple addition of a profits variable to a stock adjustment model producing an equation in which old firms
theoretically respond to one variable and new firms to
another? The point is that aggregate investment models of
the sector as a whole must be related to actual behavior by
individual firms if they are to have any meaning, and the
addition of variables to an aggregate equation to account
for heterogeneous responses by different firms is simply an
acknowledgment that aggregate analysis is not appropriate.

Regional disparities in investment behavior were clearly important in the period from 1870 to 1914, and a simple regional expansion model explains much of the observed variance in that behavior. Main track extension in the West and South was concentrated in periods of cyclical expansion, but at the individual firm level there was little direct response to pressure on existing facilities. Indeed main track extensions were more likely related to long term expectations and showed greater sensitivity to the cost of finance than to current demand pressures. In contrast investment in rolling stock and other track were closely related to increases in demand which provided very high returns to more efficient utilization of existing track. Hence total investment in track was more sensitive to demand conditions in the Northeast where other track additions were concentrated. The change in the financial climate resulting from the recovery after 1898 increased the sensitivity of all investment to the cost of investable funds. The impact was most obvious in other track additions on roads east of the Mississippi, while equipment investment was still best explained by response to shifts in demand. Financial costs were less relevant in main track extensions after 1896, and there were signs that such extensions on Western roads were more related to demand factors than they had been earlier, a trend which may well be attributed to the emergence of large systems with the prospect of increased short term returns.

Thus the principal changes in investment behavior were due to the shifting regional composition of investment and the reorganization of capital markets with a concomitant merger movement after 1898, factors which are not directly related to the age of the sector. Indeed at the firm level the cross section results indicated little change in investment behavior with age over time, although there were some interesting cyclical effects. The use of revised aggregate data clearly demonstrated that the Kmenta and Williamson life cycle results were aberrations based on the use of faulty data, and that more general models which were not related to life cycle factors produced superior results. But more importantly the company results demonstrate the fallacy of emphasizing changes in aggregate investment behavior, when there are major disparaties in the component regional patterns.

One final note on life cycles, aggregate or otherwise, should be stressed. The simple observation that investment behavior changed over time does not constitute a life cycle hypothesis. Some mechanism for the transition between the homogeneous growth stages must be proposed and the timing of transitions must be a function of age in some determinant form. Consider for example the transition mechanism between

Kmenta and Williamson's periods of "adolescence" and "ma-

turity":

> This stage (1896-1914) is characterized by expan-
> sion and consolidation of the existing firms since
> there is now very little room for opening up of
> new territories, and thus only a limited opportunity
> for new entries. The industry undergoes consider-
> able reorganization to conform to the new pattern
> of market distribution, mergers occur at a peak rate,
> and profits run at a relatively high and secularly
> stable level.[4]

Apparently the transition is defined in terms of regional

saturation in some sense, which makes entry more difficult

and stimulates major reorganizations. Abstracting from the

fact that the number of operating firms actually expanded

from 1,111 in 1896 to 1,564 in 1907, an increase of roughly

forty percent,[5] it is not at all clear why regional satura-

tion, however defined, should have the impacts attributed

to it. In point of fact the merger movement is more closely

related to the recovery of capital markets after 1898 and

the active role of banking interests, than to regional

saturation.

The issue, however, is far more than the weakness of a

single study. Analogies certainly have their place in exposi-

tion, but it is also true that they tend to develop an

---

[4]Jan Kmenta and Jeffrey Williamson, "Determinants of
Investment Behavior: United States Railroads, 1872-1941,"
Op. Cit., p. 177.

[5]Bureau of Census, Historical Statistics, Op. Cit.,
Series Q44, p. 429.

independent existence. By calling a period of early expansion "adolescence" one begins to search for signs of maturity. But if no causal links between such stages have been
developed, the force of the analogy may direct attention to
unimportant factors. This, indeed, is precisely the case in
the railroad sector from 1870 to 1914.

Methodology

The principal approach of this study was to confront
various theoretical formulations of investment behavior with
aggregate, cross section and time series data. The results
of correlation and regression analysis with the different
data sources and models were then analyzed to identify dominant statistical patterns, and compared with the available
qualitative record. The mass of data required for the analysis was staggering with roughly 21,000 company and 1,500
aggregate data elements examined in some 1,400 separate regressions. As a result the primary emphasis was on the
assembly of a large quantity of statistically significant
independent evidence which could be brought to bear on an
impartial analysis of investment behavior in the railroad
sector, rather than stressing ingenuity in the manipulation
of the data. The results of the analysis provided insights
into several methodological issues which will be related in
the following paragraphs.

Statistical and Qualitative Evidence. - - It is quite
clear that statistical correlation alone does not imply a
causal relationship between variables. When the relationship tested, however, is grounded in economic theory and a
lag structure is used which reduces simultaneous effects,
added confidence may be placed in results which correspond
to the a priori theoretical expectation. Similarly tests
for the statistical significance of particular variables are
considerably stronger when homogeneous results are obtained
from different data sources and independent decision making
units. Yet perhaps the strongest check on statistical findings is a comparison with qualitative evidence bearing on
the relationship being examined. Of course the relative
quality of the available quantitative and qualitative information will vary in different circumstances, but explorations of divergences in the results will often eliminate
the facile acceptance of apparent but misleading relationships suggested by either source. In this study the pattern
of changing investment behavior in the railroad sector suggested by an analysis of aggregate data diverged from the
implications of the available qualitative evidence. Subsequent analysis of company data revealed that the divergence
was largely due to regional disparities and produced results
which were far more consistent with the qualitative record.

Aggregate Data. - - The comparison of the statistical
results for the investment models derived from aggregate
time series data with the findings of cross section, company time series, and qualitative investigations, strongly
suggests that the sole reliance on aggregate data to distinguish among alternate investment theories in the railroad
sector from 1870 to 1914 can produce misleading conclusions.
But the two factors which combined to produce this result,
the change in investment behavior over time - which required
the analysis of small samples - and the heterogeneity of
behavior in the firms composing the aggregate, have a general impact beyond the range of this particular study.
Where structural model comparisons are required it is essential that the estimated macro relationships correspond to
homogeneous micro behavior. In cases where sectoral behavior is not homogeneous, aggregate estimates can be particularly misleading. Even when these compositional problems
are not present, small sample estimates will quite likely
be very sensitive to the precise specification of regression
models, making structural comparisons of competing models
tenuous.

Model Performance and Tests for Significance. - - A
central conclusion of the statistical results is that a sole
reliance on the R^2 as a measure of model significance can
easily lead to erroneous interpretations. In several cases,

the Klein main track model is an excellent example, apparent
changes in the significance of the model based on the R^2
were contradicted by analysis of changes in the individual
coefficients. Although the pattern of the R^2s for different
models often provided valuable insights into important changes,
there was no substitute for detailed comparisons of model coefficients in judging relative performance. In this study
primary emphasis was placed on homogeneity in the results
for different companies since, as discussed above in the use
of aggregate data, "by their very nature, structural estimates
cannot be correct if the individual micro-coefficients differ."[6] Similarly no single model has been proposed in this
study which purports to "best" explain investment behavior
in some component or period. Rather emphasis has been placed
on the performance of models measuring the influence of different types of demand and supply factors. In this way
the results are largely independent of the precise specification of any particular model. Indeed each model was examined
in preliminary analysis to determine its sensitivity to different specific formulations and variables before it was
used in more detailed analysis.

Sample Size. - - A fundamental advantage of the technique employed in this study has been a reliance on large

---

[6]Edwin Kuh, Capital Stock Growth: A Micro-Econometric
Approach, Op. Cit., p. 200.

data samples which effectively eliminates any "investigator's bias" which may be brought to the statistical analysis. Since cross section results were obtained for eighteen different samples and the time series results related to nineteen companies, it was virtually impossible to pre-judge the impact any specific modification in the models would have on the results. In the presentation of the estimates great care was taken to indicate the distribution of significant coefficients over all companies or cross sections so that average results, which could easily be misleading, were not presented out of context. Thus the degrees of freedom available for the statistical analysis were fully exploited and considerable confidence may be placed in the patterns which proved to be significant.

Perhaps the most important methodological lesson, however, lies in the limited discriminatory power of the statistical techniques which were employed. Conclusions could be drawn on variations in the importance of different types of economic factors, but there was very little success in distinguishing among the effects of particular variables such as profit and output, or gross, net, and retained earnings. Thus the statistical results demanded numerous checks with various data sources, model specifications, and even qualitative evidence before strong conclusions could be drawn.

Areas for Further Study

The results obtained in this study suggest that the
technique of combining cross section and company time series
data in an analysis of investment behavior can produce valuable insights. Although the requirement of examining variations in investment policy for different capital components
and periods dramatically increased the number of regression
estimates needed to test even a limited number of models,
the findings clarified important changes and divergences
in investment behavior. Aggregate analysis of investment
patterns, on the other hand, produced misleading results
due to disparities in the behavior of the underlying decision making units.

However, despite the substantial returns to this
initial statistical foray it is doubtful that further extension of the technique for the railroad sector as a whole
in this period would add significantly to the understanding
of investment behavior. The observed cyclic and period
variations in investment patterns suggest that extensive
cross section analysis is the only way to produce more precise distinctions in investment behavior. In particular,
regional cross sections are probably needed to reduce the
observed variation of cross section and time series results
for track investment. But consecutive cross sections are
required to trace dynamic changes, and such an analysis of

a larger sample would require a major effort of compiling
and manipulating the relevant data. There might, however,
be substantial returns to analysis of individual regions
over more limited time periods. In particular the conclusions of this study suggest that much remains to be learned
about track investment in the West and South prior to 1895.

The data which have been assembled for this analysis
of investment behavior could easily be applied to a study
of production relationships, particularly since the derived
capital series were based on production function considerations. One important step remains, however, before such an
analysis may be conducted. The available labor data apply
to the number of men employed rather than efficiency equivalent man-hour services. Much remains to be learned about
the changing productivity of the labor force and its impact
on the railroad sector. One lesson of this study cogently
applies to such an analysis of changing productivity: regional disparities will undoubtedly have an important impact
on observed production relationships, and a sole reliance
on aggregate data could easily produce misleading results.
Homogeneous regional cross sections or time series for individual companies should provide far more appropriate
vehicles for such analysis.

Beyond these specific extensions for the railroad sector in the period from 1870 to 1914, this study suggests

that similar explorations of investment or production relationships at the region or firm level could produce valuable
insights for other sectors as well. Of course the railroad
sector is unique in the wealth of statistical data it provides in such early periods. However the central conclusion
of this study is that such disaggregation may well be essential to understand important behavioral patterns, and that
a reliance on aggregate data may easily produce misleading
conclusions.

RAILROAD OUTPUT AND REVENUE 1870-1914

Introduction

Measures of output and earnings for United States railroads were desired as inputs to regression analysis and as
central variables in the overview of the industry in Chapter II. Gross and net operating revenue were available from
Poor's Manual of Railroads back to 1872, but adjustments for
coverage and linkage with later ICC data were required. The
output record was less complete with Poor's coverage of
passenger and freight mileage beginning in 1882. The development of an output index for the entire period required the
estimation of passenger-miles and freight ton-miles for 1870
to 1882 along with corresponding freight and passenger rates.

Revenue

Poor's gross and net operating revenue estimates do not
trace the annual variations accurately, since the coverage
of the series increased over time. To compensate for this
variation the ratio of total mileage reported in operation
to the mileage reporting earnings was used to adjust the

annual earnings data.[1] Since earnings were probably lower
on non-reporting roads this correction should produce an
upper bound earnings estimate. In 1890 ICC earnings data
became available and were used thereafter.[2] The Poor and
ICC data for 1890 were roughly comparable and a simple
average of the two figures was used to produce the 1890
estimate. In the case of net earnings the 1891 ICC figure
was adjusted to preserve the trend after averaging the 1890
estimates. For 1870 and 1871 gross and net earnings from
a 15 road sample were scaled to an aggregate estimate by the
ratio of scaled Poor earnings to sample earnings from 1872
to 1890 - 3.15. The input data and final gross and net
revenue series are depicted in Table Al.

Output

Harold Barger's annual output estimates based on ICC
data extend back to 1890 and are generally considered to be
the best available.[3] Poor's Manual of Railroads began

---

[1]Henry V. Poor, Manual of the Railroads, as revised by
the ICC and cited by U.S. Bureau of Census, Historical Statistics of the United States (Washington: GPO, 1960),
Series Q 23 and Q 27, p. 428. For mileage covered see Ibid,
p. 423.

[2]Interstate Commerce Commission, Statistics of Railroads in the United States, as cited by U.S. Bureau of Census, Historical Statistics, Op. Cit., Series Q 106 and Q 112,
p. 434.

[3]Harold Barger, Output in the Transportation Industries,
1889 to 1946, as cited by U.S. Bureau of Census, Historical
Statistics, Op. Cit., Series Q 12, p. 427.

Table A1

GROSS AND NET RAILROAD REVENUE 1870-1914

(Millions of Current Dollars)

Year	1	2	3	4	5	Year	4	5
1870				394	139	1890	1086	342
1871				403	142	1891	1097	344
1872	465	166	1.15	535	191	1892	1171	358
1873	526	184	1.06	558	195	1893	1220	358
1874	520	190	1.04	541	198	1894	1073	305
1875	503	186	1.03	518	194	1895	1075	311
1876	497	186	1.05	522	195	1896	1150	339
1877	472	171	1.07	505	183	1897	1222	328
1878	490	188	1.04	521	196	1898	1247	387
1879	526	217	1.10	579	239	1899	1314	412
1880	614	256	1.14	670	292	1900	1487	481
1881	702	272	1.11	779	302	1901	1599	511
1882	770	280	1.09	839	305	1902	1726	560
1883	824	298	1.10	906	328	1903	1901	590
1884	777	271	1.05	816	285	1904	1975	579
1885	773	269	1.02	788	274	1905	2082	633
1886	830	301	1.02	847	307	1906	2326	720
1887	940	335	1.09	1024	365	1907	2589	777
1888	960	302	1.03	989	311	1908	2441	635
1889	1002	322	1.01	1012	325	1909	2473	710
						1910	2812	805
						1911	2853	745
						1912	2906	727
						1913	3193	805
						1914	3128	674

Column	Description
Year	Figures are for June 30 of the year listed.
1	Gross railroad revenue from Poor's Manual of the Railroads as cited by Bureau of the Census, Historical Statistics, Op. Cit., Series Q23 plus Series Q27, p. 428.

Table A1 (Continued)

Column	Description
2	Net operating revenue taken from Ibid, Series Q40, p. 428.
3	Poor's Manual coverage index computed as the ratio of reported track mileage operated to track mileage for which earnings data were received. Figures were taken from Ibid, Series Q48, p. 429, and Table I, p. 423.
4	Adjusted gross earnings. Figures for 1870 and 1871 were derived by scaling earnings for a fifteen road sample to a national estimate by the ratio of sample to national earnings over the period from 1872 to 1890. For 1872 to 1889 the figures are the product of columns 1 and 3. For 1891 to 1914 the figures are from the Interstate Commerce Commission, Statistics of Railroads in the United States, as cited by Bureau of the Census, Historical Statistics, Op. Cit., Series Q106, p. 434. The 1890 figure is an average of the scaled Poor estimate and the ICC figure.
5	Adjusted net operating earnings. The derivation followed the procedure outlined in the note to column 4. Net operating earnings after 1890 are found in Ibid, Series Q112, p. 434. The figure for 1891 was produced by interpolation between the averaged figure for 1890 and the ICC estimate for 1892 with respect to the ICC series.

publishing aggregate passenger-mile and freight ton-mile
estimates in 1882 and those figures formed the basis of
Melville Ulmer's extension of Barger's series back to
1880.[4] A 15 road sample was used to check the annual variation in the Ulmer series and extend the estimates back to
1870. Passenger-miles and freight ton-miles reported by
the 15 roads in the sample were scaled to an industry
estimate by the ratio of industry to sample gross earnings.
Annual passenger and freight rate estimates were obtained
by interpolating between Fishlow's 1870 and 1880 rate estimates with reference to an average of rates reported by a
13 road sample.[5] The rate estimates for 1870 and 1880 differed from Fishlow's by only three percent, but his estimates were drawn from a larger sample and were taken as
benchmarks.

Table A2 presents the annual estimates of aggregate
ton-miles, passenger-miles, and passenger and ton-mile
rates. The separate output and rate data were checked by
using them to compute an independent estimate of annual
gross earnings for the period from 1870 to 1890. The close
correspondence of the estimated series shown in column 9 is
striking and adds support to the validity of the component

---

[4]Melville Ulmer, Capital in Transportation, Communications and Public Utilities, Op. Cit., p. 474.

[5]Albert Fishlow, "Productivity and Technological Change
in the Railroad Sector," Op. Cit., p. 585.

Table A2

AGGREGATE TON-MILES, PASSENGER-MILES, AND RATE ESTIMATES

1870-1890

Fiscal Year	1	2	3	4	5	6	7	8	9
1870	119	394	4.06	1.25	13.9	3.59	2.18	2.80	404
1871	122	403	4.48	1.25	14.6	4.16	2.16	2.71	430
1872	151	535	5.24	1.50	17.3	4.95	2.16	2.73	510
1873	164	558	5.99	1.71	19.2	5.47	2.15	2.65	557
1874	165	541	6.74	1.65	22.2	5.44	2.10	2.64	608
1875	156	518	6.95	1.65	23.8	5.63	1.95	2.60	609
1876	157	522	7.54	1.97	25.2	5.92	1.72	2.54	581
1877	148	505	7.63	1.57	26.8	5.51	1.59	2.50	563
1878	157	521	9.01	1.52	28.7	4.81	1.46	2.51	540
1879	164	579	10.85	1.61	36.9	5.48	1.30	2.48	616
1880	211	670	12.35	1.93	37.9	5.82	1.29	2.51	633
1881	237	779	14.16	2.27	43.6	7.00	1.24	2.50	716
1882	237	839	14.90	2.66	50.5	9.00	1.23	2.42	839
1883	272	906	16.50	2.92	53.2	9.40	1.19	2.38	858
1884	260	816	16.93	2.97	54.8	9.60	1.15	2.29	849
1885	252	788	17.79	3.21	55.7	10.05	1.07	2.16	814
1886	271	847	19.26	3.36	58.0	10.12	1.07	2.16	839
1887	298	1024	21.65	3.63	70.0	11.40	1.04	2.20	989
1888	303	989	23.01	3.94	74.4	12.70	.95	2.10	966
1889	317	1012	23.48	4.11	73.5	12.85	.94	2.18	973
1890	346	1086	26.87	4.37	82.1	13.35	.94	2.17	1047

Column	Description
1	Gross earnings of the fifteen road sample in millions of current dollars.
2	Gross earnings for all United States railroads in millions of current dollars taken from Table A1, column 4.
3	Total ton-miles of freight carried by the fifteen road sample in billions.
4	Total passenger-miles carried by the fifteen road sample in billions.

Table A2 (Continued)

Column   Description

5   Aggregate ton-miles estimate in billions computed
         as column 3 times the ratio of column 2 to
         column 1.

6   Aggregate passenger-miles estimate in billions com-
         puted as column 4 times the ratio of column 2
         to column 1.

7   Gross revenue per ton-mile in current cents. For
         1870 and 1880 the rates are from Albert Fishlow,
         "Productivity and Technological Change in the
         Railroad Sector," Op. Cit., p. 585. The 1890
         rate is from the Interstate Commerce Commission,
         Statistics of Railways in the United States, as
         cited by Bureau of the Census, Historical Stat-
         istics, Series Q 86, p. 431. Annual figures
         were derived by interpolation between those
         bench marks with respect to the average rate
         reported by a thirteen road sample.

8   Gross revenue per passenger-mile in current cents,
         computed as outlined in the note to column 7.
         The ICC rate for 1890 is found in Ibid, Series
         Q72, p. 430.

9   Gross earnings in millions of current dollars,
         derived as gross passenger earnings (column 4
         times column 8) plus gross freight earnings
         (column 3 times column 7). This series may
         be used as a check on the component output and
         rate estimates by comparison with gross earn-
         ings derived in Table A1, column 4, and re-
         peated as column 2 of this table.

series. The aggregate component estimates were converted
to a link relative index of output. The link relative index
was chosen due to the changing composition of output between passenger and ton miles over time in an effort to
avoid the bias resulting from the selection of a single base
year. One index was computed for the entire period from
1870 to 1890 for comparison with Ulmer's series, and a
second index was developed for 1870 to 1880.

Table A3 portrays the resulting series, links the results with Barger's estimates, and compares the results with
a separate estimate by Fishlow. The Ulmer series shows a
slightly larger increase in output through the 1880s than
the sample estimates, but the results are very similar.
Since the Ulmer series had a broader data base it was ac-
cepted as a reasonable portrayal of output variations back
to 1880. The sample results were used to extend the series
back to 1870 and the resulting estimates are shown in column
4 of Table A3. The final series closely follows the decadal
pattern derived by Fishlow. Annual estimates of output in
1910 dollars were derived by multiplying Ulmer's 1910 output
estimate by the link relative index.

Summary

The extension of output and earnings data for the railroad sector back to 1870 was accomplished by adjusting the
existing Poor series for coverage and estimating earlier

Table A3

COMPARISON OF OUTPUT INDEXES 1870-1914

Year	1	2	3	4	5	6	Year	4	5	6
1870	17.9	40.5	5.6	5.4	6.0	134	1891	34.0		844
1871	19.7	44.4	6.2	5.9		146	1892	36.4		903
1872	23.3	52.6	6.3	7.0		174	1893	38.6		958
1873	25.9	58.4	8.2	7.8		194	1894	34.6		859
1874	28.8	65.0	9.1	8.7		215	1895	35.0		869
1875	30.4	68.7	9.6	9.2		228	1896	38.7		961
1876	32.1	72.4	10.1	9.7		241	1897	37.9		941
1877	33.0	74.4	10.4	9.8		243	1898	44.5		1104
1878	34.3	77.4	10.8	10.3		256	1899	48.3		1199
1879	42.9	96.8	13.5	12.9		320	1900	54.6	54.8	1355
1880	44.3	100.0	14.0	13.3	13.8	330	1901	57.1		1417
1881	51.6		16.6	15.4		382	1902	61.9		1536
1882	61.4		19.3	16.6		412	1903	67.6		1679
1883	64.3		20.2	18.5		459	1904	68.8		1708
1884	67.6		21.3	15.7		390	1905	74.0		1837
1885	71.4		22.5	20.4		506	1906	83.9		2082
1886	72.6		22.8	21.8		541	1907	92.0		2283
1887	86.0		27.1	25.0		621	1908	86.9		2157
1888	92.5		29.1	26.5		658	1909	86.9		2157
1889	91.4		28.8	28.0		695	1910	100.0	100.0	2482
1890	100.0		31.5	31.5	32.8	782	1911	100.2		2487
							1912	103.3		2564
							1913	115.0		2854
							1914	112.6		2795

Column	Description
Year	Data are for June 30 of the year listed.
1	Link relative index, 1890=100, based on data in Table A2.
2	Link relative index, 1880=100, based on data in Table A2.
3	Output index, 1910=100, derived by linking column 1 to Harold Barger's index, Output in the Transportation Industries, NBER (Princeton: Princeton University Press, 1951), Appendix B, in 1890.

Table A3 (Continued)

Column   Description

4   Output index, 1910=100, derived by linking column
         2 to Melville Ulmer's index, Capital in Trans-
         portation, Op. Cit., p. 474, in 1880 and to
         Barger's index in 1890.

5   Link relative index, 1910=100, from Albert Fishlow,
         "Productivity and Technological Change in the
         Railroad Sector," Op. Cit., p. 585.

6   Output in millions of 1910 dollars, derived as
         column 4 times $2,482 million, the 1910 out-
         put estimate derived by Ulmer, Capital in
         Transportation, Op. Cit., p.472, adjusted to
         1910 from 1929 dollars using his price index
         on pp. 276-277.

figures from a fifteen road sample. Separate estimates of
passenger-miles, freight ton-miles, and passenger and
freight rates were found to be consistent with estimates
of gross earnings. The link relative output series computed
from the derived data was quite similar to Ulmer's alternate
annual estimates for the 1880s and Fishlow's decadal benchmarks. The internal consistency of the data and support
from external comparisons add credence to the validity of
the derived series.

RAILROAD EMPLOYMENT 1870-1914

Introduction

Employment figures played a peripheral role in the
analysis of investment, but they were derived as part of the
overview of changing productivity in the railroad sector examined in Chapter II. ICC employment estimates became available in 1891, but no annual employment estimates are available for the period from 1870 to 1890. In an effort to
derive annual estimates for this early period two steps were
required: (1) the derivation of reliable benchmark estimates at short enough intervals to accurately trace the
trend of employment, (2) the establishment of a strong relationship between employment and some known aggregate variable
for interpolation between the benchmark years.

Estimates

The Census data available for 1880[1] and 1890[2] may be
taken as reliable decadal benchmarks, but the Census of

---

[1]Tenth Census, 1880, Vol. IV, Report on the Agencies of
Transportation in the United States (Washington: GPO, 1883),
p. 130-137.

[2]Eleventh Census, 1890, Vol. III, Report on the Trans-
ortation Business in the United States (Washington: GPO,
895), pp. 257-279.

Occupations for 1870 was notably incomplete. Alternate estimates produced by Fishlow,[3] Lebergott,[4] and Carson[5] are available for 1870, but they are remarkably inconsistent. Lebergott's estimate of 159,120 was derived by scaling employment from company and state reports to a national estimate by the ratio of national to sample track mileage. However, Fishlow has challenged his low estimate for the Middle Atlantic region and the implied high rate of employment growth in that region from 1870 to 1880.[6] Carson adjusted the available Census data by the degree of under-coverage observed in later years and achieved a much higher employment estimate of 270,223 for 1870. The degree of undercoverage was not stable, however, and if the average level of undercoverage implied by Carson's figures, .60, is substituted for his estimate of .57, the resulting employment estimate is reduced to 256,550. More confidence could be placed in Carson's estimate if a stable trend of coverage could be established. Fishlow used a company

---

[3]Albert Fishlow, "Productivity and Technological Change in the Railroad Sector," Op. Cit., p. 613.

[4]Stanley Lebergott, Manpower in Economic Growth (New York: 1964), p. 512.

[5]Daniel Carson, "Changes in the Industrial Composition of Manpower since the Civil War," Income and Wealth, Vol II, NBER (New York: Columbia University Press, 1949), pp. 46-134.

[6]Albert Fishlow, "Productivity and Technological Change in the Railroad Sector," Op. Cit., p. 617.

sample scaled by the ratio of national to sample gross earnings to obtain an estimate of 230,000, after demonstrating that a strong cross-section correlation existed between earnings and employment.

To develop an independent estimate of employment for 1870 and establish additional benchmarks for 1875 and 1885 annual State Railroad Commission reports were examined.[7] The ratios of employment to gross earnings in the samples were used to derive aggregate employment estimates. Interpolation between these benchmark years was accomplished with reference to the annual series of gross earnings in Table A1. Eight sample companies which reported employment and gross earnings through most of the period were used to test the assumption that employment levels were correlated with gross earnings over time. The results of the regressions shown in Table B1 indicate that a close relationship exists between employment and earnings and support the contention that earnings are a suitable vehicle for the interpolation of employment.

---

[7]For the reports included in each sample see the notes to Table B2.

Table B1

ORDINARY LEAST SQUARES REGRESSION OF EMPLOYMENT ON EARNINGS
FOR SELECTED COMPANIES

Company	Period	Coefficient (t)	R^2
Boston & Maine	1871-1911	.66(49.2)	.98
New York, New Haven, & Hartford	1869-1910	.63(39.2)	.97
Pennsylvania	1879-1909	.62(31.2)	.97
Chicago & Northwestern	1878-1909	.58(25.3)	.95
Chicago, Burlington, & Quincy	1879-1909	.47(19.3)	.92
Michigan Central	1873-1909	.57(18.1)	.90
Union Pacific	1879-1909	.49(29.2)	.96
Atchison, Topeka, & Santa Fe	1879-1908	.17(7.2)	.91

The estimates of annual employment levels are presented in Table B2. As a test of the technique 1880 employment was estimated by interpolating between the sample benchmark estimates for 1875 and 1885 with respect to gross earnings. The resulting estimate of 398,887 is only 4.8 percent lower than the Census figure of 418,957. This is encouraging since both benchmarks were independently derived by the scaling technique and the ten year span does not catch the variation in the trend of employment as accurately as the five year periods actually used in interpolation.

The 1870 estimate of 238,000 falls between Carson's 270,223 and Fishlow's 230,000. The similarity of the sample results with Fishlow's estimate is due in part to the reliance on similar scaling techniques and, since the State

Table B2

ANNUAL RAILROAD EMPLOYMENT 1870-1914

Year	1	2	3	Year	3
1870	.649	394	238	1891	784
1871		403	241	1892	821
1872		499	273	1893	874
1873		525	281	1894	780
1874		544	288	1895	785
1875	.533	532	284	1896	827
1876		525	276	1897	823
1877		519	269	1898	875
1878		501	246	1899	929
1879		559	335	1900	1018
1880	(.647)	649	419	1901	1071
1881		730	487	1902	1189
1882		802	548	1903	1313
1883		877	611	1904	1296
1884		841	580	1905	1382
1885	.681	790	538	1906	1521
1886		817	560	1907	1672
1887		965	679	1908	1436
1888		979	690	1909	1503
1889		991	701	1910	1699
1890	(.712)	1052	750	1911	1670
				1912	1716
				1913	1815
				1914	1710

Column	Description
Year	Figures are for June 30 of the year listed.
1	The ratio of sample employment in thousands to sample gross earnings in millions of current dollars. The samples included annual reports from state railroad commissions as follows: 1870 - Virginia, Massachusetts, Ohio, Connecticut; 1875 - Pennsylvania, Connecticut, Michigan, Massachusetts, Wisconsin, Virginia; 1885 - Pennsylvania, Kansas, Connecticut, Indiana, Massachusetts, Nebraska, Michigan, and Dakota. Figures in parentheses are the ratio of Census data in column 3 to gross earnings in column 2.

Table B2 (Continued)

Column   Description

2   Gross earnings in millions of current dollars
               from Table A1.

3   Annual railroad employment in thousands. For
               1880 and 1890 data are from the United States
               Census as listed in footnotes 1 and 2. For
               1870, 1875, and 1885 employment is computed
               as coulmn 1 times column 2. For all other
               years from 1870 to 1890 the employment figures
               are derived by interpolation with respect to
               column 2. For 1891 to 1914 figures are taken
               from the Interstate Commerce Commission,
               Statistics of Railways in the United States,
               as cited by Bureau of the Census, Historical
               Statistics, Op. Cit., Series Q141, p. 437.

Commission reports undoubtedly included some of Fishlow"s
sample companies, the use of only partially independent
samples. On the other hand the results do add some weight
to Fishlow's estimate, particularly when coupled with the
earlier observation that Carson's estimate may be high.

Summary

The estimation techniques used to derive employment
figures from 1870 to 1890 were developed around established
behavioral relationships. Independent techniques were de-
vised to establish firm semi-decadal benchmarks and to interpolate between those benchmarks. A test of the technique
for 1880 suggested that the results were still reasonably
accurate when a ten year span was used for interpolation.
The consistency of the result for 1870 with the analysis of
the alternate employment estimates provided further support
for the trend of the derived series.

APPENDIX C

RAILROAD CAPITAL PRICE INDEX 1370-1914

Introduction

The estimation of price indexes for track and equipment,
as well as a combined index of track and equipment, over a
44 year period is a formidable task. The normal index
number problem is accentuated by a scarcity of relevant
price data, dramatic technical changes in each capital component, and a marked shift in the composition of investment
over time. In addition, significant regional price variations may be anticipated in a period of rapid territorial
expansion and market disequilibrium. The available price
data are not sufficient to adequately compensate for each of
these sources of bias, but reasonable estimates as to the
direction and the extent of each bias can be made. The remainder of this appendix outlines the derivation of separate
price indexes for track and equipment, discusses the formulation of a combined index of track and equipment, explores
the extent of regional price variations, and compares the
results with the findings of other studies of price variations in the railroad sector in this period.

Track

The annual cost of track construction per mile was derived by multiplying an estimate of the 1910 cost of track
per mile by a combined index of the prices of the three
principal construction inputs: (1) construction materials,
(2) rail, (3) wages. The Warren and Pearson index of wholesale building materials was selected as the best proxy for
railroad construction materials.[1] Iron and steel prices
were taken from Temin for 1870 to 1890 and weighted by the
annual percentage of iron and steel rails produced domesti-
cally to form a single rail index.[2] After 1890 steel rail
prices were taken from the American Metal Market and Daily
Iron and Steel Report.[3] Annual ICC statistical reports of
the wages of "other trackmen" were used for construction
wages from 1890 to 1914.[4] Lebergott's "non-farm" labor
decadal wage benchmarks were used to establish the wage

[1]George F. Warren and Frank A. Pearson, Gold and Prices
(New York: John Wiley and Sons, 1935), p. 31.

[2]Peter Temin, Iron and Steel in Nineteenth-Century
America (Cambridge, Mass.: MIT Press, 1964), pp. 273, 284.

[3]United States Bureau of the Census, Historical Statistics of the United States, Historical Times to 1957
(Washington: GPO, 1960), Series E108, p. 123.

[4]Interstate Commerce Commission, Annual Statistics of
Railroads in the United States for 1890 to 1914 (Washington:
GPO, 1891 to 1915).

trend from 1870 to 1890,[5] while annual estimates were produced by interpolation with respect to the unskilled wage
series in Bulletin 18 of the Department of Labor.[6] The
latter series is composed of wage quotations for fourteen
unskilled occupations in twelve large cities and is generally considered as higher than the national average.[7] Since
the larger cities provided a labor pool for railroad construction workers, particularly in the form of immigrant
labor, and a higher wage would be expected for those drawn
off into the railroad sector, the series should provide a
reasonable vehicle for interpolation.

An obvious correction to the wage data would be some
compensation for increasing labor productivity over time.
The brief analysis of total factor productivity in Chapter
II suggests that such a correction would be significant for
all railroad labor. A detailed analysis of increasing spe-
cialization of tasks in road construction crews might shed
considerable light on the magnitude and trend of an

---

[5]Stanley Lebergott, "Wage Trends 1800-1900," Trends in
the American Economy in the 19th Century, National Bureau of
Economic Research (Princeton: Princeton University Press,
1960), p. 482.

[6]Carroll D. Wright (ed), Bulletin 18, Dept. of Labor,
1898, as cited by Clarence D. Long, Wages and Earnings in
the United States, 1860-1890, NBER (Princeton: Princeton
University Press, 1960), Table A-4, p. 135.

[7]Compared with the Dewey Census Report for 1890 and the
First Annual Report of the Commission of Labor, 1884, as
cited by Clarence D. Long, Ibid, p. 602.

appropriate correction. At this juncture, however, compensation for changing productivity must be limited to the observation that wage data understate the decline of wages in terms of constant efficiency units and overstate wage increases.

The disparate movements of the three construction input price series suggest that the weights assigned to each series will significantly affect the trend of the track price index. Table C1 traces the pattern of the input series. The building materials series falls quite uniformly from 1870 to 1900, and then rises through 1914. The rail index falls rapidly from 1870 to 1885, remains steady from 1885 to 1900, and then rises through 1914. The linked series of construction wages falls slightly from 1870 to 1890 and then rises until 1914. The critical factor in the construction of a combined input series is the weight assigned to the rail index because of its sharp fall from 1870 to 1885.

The weights applied to each input series were estimated from an analysis of state railroad commission reports which contained a breakdown of road construction data. Three year periods were selected to smooth annual variations, and three state commission reports were examined in each period.[8] The

---

[8] Annual Railroad Commission Reports for New York (1874-1876, 1896-1898), Massachusetts (1874-1876, 1885-1887, 1896-1898), Michigan (1874-1876, 1885-1887, 1896-1898), and Dakota Territory (1885-1887).

Table C1

TRACK INPUT PRICE SERIES 1870-1914

Year	1	2	3	4	5	6	7	8
1870	1.32	90	101	72.35	106.75	6	74.33	265
1871	1.29	88	102	70.38	102.50	5	72.01	257
1872	1.30	88	107	85.13	112.00	9	87.52	314
1873	1.31	89	106	76.67	120.50	14	82.83	296
1874	1.27	86	101	58.75	94.25	20	65.90	235
1875	1.28	87	90	47.75	68.75	37	55.57	198
1876	1.26	86	84	41.25	59.25	47	49.76	178
1877	1.11	76	80	35.25	45.50	56	40.99	146
1878	1.09	74	72	33.75	42.25	62	39.10	140
1879	1.09	74	74	41.25	48.25	62	45.64	163
1880	1.08	74	81	49.25	67.50	66	61.31	219
1881	1.11	76	83	47.13	61.13	73	57.32	205
1882	1.18	80	88	45.50	48.50	87	48.12	172
1883	1.19	81	85		37.75	95	37.75	135
1884	1.18	80	84		30.75	97	30.75	110
1885	1.17	80	81		28.50	99	28.50	104
1886	1.17	80	82		34.50		34.50	125
1887	1.18	80	81		37.08		37.08	132
1888	1.17	80	80		29.83		29.83	107
1889	1.16	79	81		29.25		29.25	104
1890	1.18	80	84				31.78	114
1891	1.20	82	80				29.92	107
1892	1.22	83	76				30.00	107
1893	1.22	83	75				28.13	100
1894	1.18	80	72				24.00	86
1895	1.17	80	70				24.33	86
1896	1.17	80	70				28.00	100
1897	1.16	79	68				18.75	68
1898	1.16	79	72				17.63	64
1899	1.18	80	79				28.13	100
1900	1.22	83	84				32.29	115
1901	1.23	84	80				27.33	100
1902	1.25	85	82				28.00	100
1903	1.31	89	85				28.00	100
1904	1.33	90	82				28.00	100
1905	1.32	90	87				28.00	100
1906	1.36	93	98				28.00	100
1907	1.46	99	103				28.00	100

Table C1 (Continued)

Year	1	2	3	7	8
1908	1.45	99	94	28.00	100
1909	1.38	94	97	28.00	100
1910	1.47	100	100	28.00	100
1911	1.50	102	100	28.00	100
1912	1.50	102	101	28.00	100
1913	1.58	107	103	30.00	107
1914	1.59	108	96	30.00	107

Column   Description

Year   Fiscal year.

1   Daily wage of construction workers in dollars per
        hour. See text for sources and derivation.

2   Index of construction wages, 1910=100. Column
        1 divided by 1.47, the 1910 daily wage.

3   Materials price index, 1910=100, using the ratio
        of annual to 1910 prices from George F. Warren
        and Frank A. Pearson, Gold and Prices, Op. Cit.,
        p. 31.

4   Price of iron rail at Pennsylvania works in dol-
        lars per ton from Peter Temin, Iron and Steel
        in Nineteenth-Century America, Op. Cit., p. 284.

5   Price of bessemer steel rail at Pennsylvania mills
        in dollars per ton from Temin, Ibid.

6   The ratio of domestic steel rail production to all
        rail production from Temin, Ibid.

7   Index of the price of rail weighting steel and iron
        rail prices by the proportions of steel and iron
        rail produced domestically. After 1882 this is
        simply the price of steel rail.

8   Index of the price of rail, 1910=100 computed as
        the ratio of column 7 to the price of rail in
        1910.

results for each sample are depicted in Table C2, and compared with independent estimates compiled by Fishlow for
1851 to 1860,[9] a chief engineer of the Illinois Central for
1897,[10] and the ICC for 1918.[11] The consistency of the
estimates suggest that the trends depicted are substantially
correct. The increasing percentage of building materials is
consistent with the increasing complexity of the materials
used in construction exemplified by the shift from earth and
cinder ballast to stone and gravel.[12] The decreasing percentage of rail is consistent with the dramatic price reductions throughout the period, and the constant labor share
is supported by the lack of major labor saving innovations
in construction.

To explore the impact of the selection of a base year
on the resulting track price index two indexes were developed.
The first was computed with an 1875 base using the weights
for the three input series derived from the 1874 to 1876

---

[9]Albert Fishlow, American Railroads and the Transformation of the Ante-Bellum Economy (Cambridge, Mass.: Harvard
University Press, 1965), p. 351.

[10]A. M. Van Auken, "Preliminary Investigation of New
Railway Projects," Railway Age Gazette (March 8, 1912), pp.
427-429.

[11]Interstate Commerce Commission, Statistics of the
Railroads in the United States for 1918, Op. Cit., p. 87.

[12]Bruce V. Crandall, Track Labor Cost Data (Chicago:
Lytton, 1920), p. 27.

Table C2

PER CENT OF TRACK COST BY COMPONENT

Component	1	2	3	4	5	6
Rail	30	35	25	20	25	22
Building Materials	10	5	15	20	15	15
Construction Wages	60	60	60	60	60	63

Column	Description
1	1851-1860. Derived by Albert Fishlow, American Railroads and the Transformation of the Ante-Bellum Economy, Op. Cit., p. 351.
2	1874-1876. Computed from railroad commission annual reports from New York, Michigan and Massachusetts.
3	1885-1887. Computed from railroad commission annual reports from Michigan, Dakota and Massachusetts.
4	1896-1898. Computed from railroad commission annual reports from New York, Michigan, and Massachusetts.
5	1897. Estimate produced by an engineer of the Illinois Central as cited by A. M. Van Auken, "Preliminary Investigation of Railroad Projects," Railway Age Gazette (March 8, 1912), pp. 427-429.
6	1918. Interstate Commerce Commission, Statistics of the Railroads in the United States for 1918, Op. Cit., p. 87.

sample. The second was computed with a 1910 base using weights of .22 for rail, .16 for building materials, and .62 for wages. The resulting indexes are shown in Table C3. After the initial disparity in 1870 and 1875 the two series quickly converged. Since the 1874 to 1876 weight for track falls above the trend indicated by the sources for other years, the use of a 1910 base should not result in a serious distortion of the magnitude or the trend of the track price index.

Equipment

Separate prices for locomotives, freight cars, and passenger cars were desired to simplify the corrections for changing component efficiency and as inputs to the derivation of annual investment data in Appendix D. Unfortunately equipment prices were rarely reported in the detail required for accurate interpretation. Company reports frequently listed expenditures for new equipment by component, but models were rarely given. The comparison of such general data among companies over time is hazardous, but recourse to other sources is also limited. The most comprehensive study of equipment prices was produced by Shaw in Value of Commodity Output Since 1869, but his figures are aggregated for all locomotives and cars and are available

Table C3

COMPARISON OF PRICE INDEXES

Year	1	2	3	4	5	6	7	8
1870	98.2	33.4	81.8	89.9	35.4	99.3		86.8
1875	89.7	33.6	75.5	82.5	34.9	90.6		85.0
1880	85.8	32.5	72.3	82.8	32.7	91.3		75.2
1885	76.9	35.1	66.4	69.0	34.0	74.9		73.6
1890	81.1	42.6	71.4	75.3	42.2	80.9		73.2
1895	76.1	50.6	69.7	72.3	51.4	75.9		66.5
1900	85.0	74.8	82.4	84.6	76.7	85.9	87.7	77.5
1905	93.5	98.3	94.7	96.6	99.4	96.1	90.3	84.8
1910	100.0	100.0	100.0	100.0	100.0	100.0	100.0	100.0
1914	105.9	102.8	105.1	106.4	102.8	107.1	99.2	101.1

Column	Description
Year	Fiscal year.
1	Track price index, 1910=100, using the 1910 weights of .22 for rail, .16 for materials, and .62 for wages.
2	Equipment price index, 1910=100, using 1910 purchases of locomotives, freight cars and passenger cars as weights for component prices.
3	Track and equipment price index, 1910=100, weighting each component by its proportion of 1910 investment.
4-6	The same as columns 1-3 respectively except the relative weights for 1875 replaced those for 1910.
7	Railroad capital price index from Larry Neal, "Investment Behavior by American Railroads: 1897-1914," Op. Cit., p. 132, adjusted to a 1910 base.
8	Railroad capital price index from Melville Ulmer, Capital in Transportation, Op. Cit., pp. 290-291, adjusted to a 1910 base.

only after 1888.[13] Earlier decadal benchmarks are provided
by Brady for 1869 through 1899, but her figures are also
composites for both locomotives and cars and contradict the
trend for 1889 to 1899 given by Shaw.[14] Census data by component are available for 1899 and 1909, but only locomotive
prices are given for 1889.

In order to interpret price data which were available
from a wide variety of sources for difference years and
equipment models, separate graphs of prices versus weight
by model or year were plotted for locomotives, passenger
cars, and freight cars.[15] Only data for coach passenger
cars and standard box freight cars were used. The

_____

[13]William H. Shaw, Value of Commodity Output Since 1869,
NBER (New York: 1947), p. 294.

[14]Dorothy Brady, "Price Deflators for Final Product
Estimates," Output, Employment, and Productivity in the
United States after 1800, NBER (New York: Columbia Univer-
sity Press, 1966), p. 211.

[15]Equipment price citations from the Annual Reports of
the New York Central, the Chicago, Milwaukee and St. Paul,
and the Michigan Central were used throughout the period. In
addition the following sources were used by component:
Locomotives: Albert Fishlow, "Productivity and Techno-
logical Change in the Railroad Sector," Op. Cit., p. 605.
A. M. Wellington, The Economic Theory of the Location of the
Railways (6th ed rev; New York: John Wiley and Sons, 1906),
pp. 411, 564. John H. White, Jr., American Locomotives: An
Engineering History: 1830-1880 (Baltimore: Johns Hopkins
Press, 1968), p. 22.
Passenger Cars: Albert Fishlow, "Productivity and Tech-
nological Change in the Railroad Sector," Op. Cit., p. 603.
A. M. Wellington, Location of the Railways, Op. Cit., p. 71.
Freight Cars: A. M. Wellington, Ibid, pp. 204-5, 486.
Albert Fishlow, "Productivity and Technological Change in
the Railroad Sector," Op. Cit., p. 603.

justification for that decision is explored in some detail
in Appendix D. The graphs were then entered with representative semi-decadal weight estimates and corresponding
prices were read for the appropriate model type. The semi-
decadal equipment weight estimates are derived in Appendix
D. Since price estimates for different years were joined
on graphs for each model the classic problem of distinguishing shifts along a curve from shifts of the weight price
relationship curves over time must be confronted. The data
are not sufficient to produce a satisfactory solution to
this dilemma, but the resulting graphical patterns, as
illustrated for locomotives in Figure C1, suggest that price
variations over time were closely related to weight changes
within model classifications. In the case of locomotives
Census data were not included in the graphical analysis and
may therefore be used to check the results of the procedure.
Table C4 compares the graphical results with the Census
estimates.[16] The graphical estimates are roughly five percent larger than the Census figures and trace the price
trend quite accurately. Therefore the semi-decadal estimates of equipment prices were used to establish the price
trend, while annual variations were derived by interpolation
with respect to the Warren and Pearson wholesale price index

---

[16]Albert Fishlow, Ibid, p. 603.

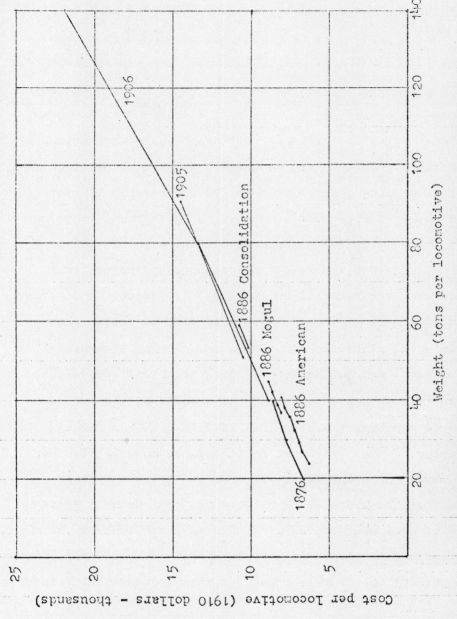

Fig. C1. -- Graph of locomotive weight vs. cost, selected dates and models

Table C4

PRICES OF NEW LOCOMOTIVES (Current Dollars)

Source	1889	1899	1909
Census	8,200	9,500	12,045
Figure C1	8,670	9,910	12,600

Row	Description
Census	Census figures for 30 June of the year listed are from Albert Fishlow, "Productivity and Technological Change in the Railroad Sector," Op. Cit., p. 603.
Figure C1	Figure C1 depicts locomotive prices as of 30 June in 1910 dollars, where current prices were deflated with a GNP price index. The graph is entered with semi-decadal weights shown in Table D4, and 1910 prices are read on an appropriate model or vintage curve. Multiplying this price by the GNP price index produces a current year price. For example the 1889 price is derived by entering Figure C1 with a weight of 51.5 tons and reading a 1910 dollar price of $10,200. Multiplying by .84, the value of the GNP price index adjusted to a 1910 base, a current dollar price of $8,670 is obtained. The GNP deflator was taken from John W. Kendrick, Productivity Trends in the United States, in Bureau of the Census, Long Term Economic Growth, 1860-1965 (Washington, D.C.: GPO, 1966), p. 200.

prior to 1888[17] and with reference to the Shaw index for locomotive and car prices from 1888 to 1914. The results are presented in Table C5.

Indexes

Thus far separate price series for track, locomotives, freight cars, and passenger cars have been developed, but the introduction to this appendix cited two major problems in combining these series into price indexes: (1) the correction for technical change in the components, (2) the bias inherent in the selection of any base period where the composition of investment shifted over time. The first problem is simply that price data do not refer to comparable commodities over time. Appendix E outlines the rapid pace of technical change in track and rolling stock. Failure to correct for this technical change would result in an over estimate of price increases and an under estimate of price declines. The second problem is the classic index number problem: the choice of a base year will determine the weights to be applied to each price series, and when the composition of expenditures is not constant different results will be obtained for different base periods. The extent of the resulting divergence in indexes with different bases

---

[17]George F. Warren and Frank A. Pearson, Gold and Prices, Op. Cit., p. 31.

Table C5

ANNUAL EQUIPMENT PRICE ESTIMATES 1870-1914 (Current Dollars)

Year	1	2	3	Year	1	2	3
1870	8570	5310	770	1900	10380	7889	637
1871	8585	5228	731	1901	11050	8054	683
1872	8600	5366	778	1902	11050	8054	683
1873	8615	5296	754	1903	11160	8233	732
1874	8630	5142	698	1904	11800	8620	810
1875	8645	4960	638	1905	12100	8810	829
1876	8502	4778	568	1906	12300	8940	840
1877	8359	4687	533	1907	12500	9060	851
1878	8216	4005	458	1908	12700	9225	866
1879	8073	3965	453	1909	12800	9300	871
1880	7930	4550	480	1910	12065	8638	843
1881	7982	4583	489	1911	12523	8966	875
1882	8034	4638	504	1912	13272	9526	927
1883	8086	4561	483	1913	12186	8724	851
1884	8138	4473	459	1914	12403	8880	867
1885	8190	4390	438				
1886	8193	4532	439				
1887	8195	4674	440				
1888	8198	4816	440				
1889	8200	4958	441				

Column	Description
Year	Figures are for June 30 of the year listed.
1	Locomotive prices. For the derivation of semi-decadal price estimates see Table C4. Annual estimates were derived by interpolation with respect to the Warren and Pearson wholesale price index in Gold and Prices, Op. Cit., p. 31, prior to 1888, and with respect to William Shaw's index of rolling stock prices in Value of Commodity Output, Op. Cit., p. 294, from 1888 to 1914.
2	Passenger car prices. See note to column 1.
3	Freight car prices. See note to column 1.

will depend on the extent of the change in the composition of expenditures and the divergence of the individual price series.

With these difficulties in mind price indexes for all equipment and for equipment plus track were developed using the following formula:

$$p = \frac{\sum_{i=1}^{n} p_{it} \, q_{ib} \, e_{it}}{\sum_{i=1}^{n} p_{ib} \, q_{ib}}$$

where p is the price index for the particular combination of capital components, p_{it} is the price of component i in year t, q_{ib} is the quantity of component i purchased in the base year, e_{it} is the performance index of component i in year t relative to the base year, p_{ib} is the price of component i in the base year, and there are n capital goods in the index. Defining

$$c_{ib} = \frac{p_{ib} \, q_{ib}}{\sum_{i=1}^{n} p_{ib} \, q_{ib}}$$

and substituting in the price index the formula becomes:

$$p = \sum_{i=1}^{n} c_{ib} \frac{p_{it}}{p_{io}} e_{it} \quad .$$

The constant c_{ib} is the proportion of total expenditures on the n capital components in the base year contributed by expenditures on component i. This proportion may be taken

directly from the gross investment figures in Appendix D.
The performance index for each component is given in
Appendix E.

To test for the sensitivity of the price indexes to the
choice of a base period the results for 1875 and 1910 bases
were compared. Table C3 gives the relevant data. The two
bases produced almost identical results for equipment, but
the 1875 base combined track and equipment index was substantially higher than the 1910 base until roughly 1900.
The latter result was not unexpected since it underscores
the increasing proportion of gross investment directed to
equipment over time. As a result the 1875 base weights the
track series more heavily than the 1910 base, and the track
series remains above the equipment series until roughly
1900. This divergence is reinforced by the variance of the
track series for the two periods due to the different weighting of the rail series, as noted above. In general the
choice of a base period appears to have little impact on
separate track and equipment indexes, but a substantial impact on a joint track and equipment index.

Since the price indexes for this study were developed
as independent variables for regression analysis to be conducted primarily by component, the finding that the base had
little impact on the separate track and equipment indexes
was encouraging. However, the result for the combined index

suggested that the selection of the base might have a distorting impact on the regression analysis. To examine this
possibility the combined 1875 index was regressed on the
1910 base index, producing the following result:

$$p_{75} = -.0781 + 1.0468 \ p_{10} \qquad R^2 = .94 \quad .$$
$$(25.8)$$

The "t" statistic is shown in parentheses under the coefficient. This result suggests that the annual variations in
the combined indexes are very similar and that the choice
of base period would not distort the regression results.

The 1910 base price indexes were selected for subsequent use in regression analysis, and are recorded in
columns 14 through 16 of Table F1. The inclusion of an
adjustment for changing capital efficiency over time should
increase the comparability of price data and minimize the
bias in the indexes due to technical change. The analysis
of indexes with different base periods indicates that the
relative bias is small for separate track and equipment
series, and that while the bias is substantial for the combined series it should not distort the regression analysis.

Regional Price Variation

The price data discussed thus far abstract from regional price variations which could be important in the
analysis of the investment decisions of individual companies.
Regional price data are difficult to obtain because of the

wide use of "cost of road and equipment" as a primary classification in railroad accounting. Regional estimates of the cost of road and equipment per mile must be adjusted for regional variations in the proportionate investment in rolling stock to obtain comparable estimates of the cost of road per mile. Unfortunately the cost of right of way is included in the cost of road figures so some adjustment for regional land costs is also required. Regional variations in equipment prices are more difficult to obtain, but were undoubtedly limited by transport costs and hence far less significant.

It is clear that any corrections to the price series to account for regional price variations would be quite crude, but are such corrections necessary? The answer depends on the degree to which prices varied over regions at one point in time, and the amount of variation in the trend of prices over time among regions. The latter question may be addressed by examining regional construction wage data reported by the ICC from 1892 to 1914.[18] Although there was little wage variation over the period the variations that occurred were essentially the same for all regions. The evidence on variations among regions at one point in time is less sanguine.

---

[18]Interstate Commerce Commission, Annual Statistics of the Railroads in the United States for 1892 through 1914, Op. Cit.

For the six regions of the 1880 Census the cost of road
per mile varied from a low of $31,600 in the Old South to a
high of $60,900 in the West.[19] Poor's Manual for 1891 cites
estimates of the book value of road and equipment for eight
regions in 1890.[20] Subtracting an estimate of the book
value of equipment to obtain the cost of road construction
alone, and dividing by the sum of main track and one-half
all other track produced a rough estimate of the cost of
road per mile in each region.[21] Eliminating the Middle
Atlantic region with an atypical cost of road per mile of
$62,000 due to high right of way and building charges, the
cost of road per mile varied from a low of $32,800 in the
South Atlantic region to a high of $57,600 in the Pacific
area. Although regional definitions changed between the
1880 Census and the 1890 Poor data, the regional differences
remained constant with the exception of New England where
the cost of road per mile apparently fell from $47,600 in

---

[19]Tenth United States Census, 1880, Volume IX, pp.
291-1.

[20]Poor's Manual of the Railroads for 1891, pp. ii-iii.

[21]An estimate of the national book value of equipment
was obtained by multiplying the cost of road and equipment
for all United States roads by the ratio of gross equipment
capital to gross equipment and track capital derived in
Appendix D. Regional equipment book value was derived by
multiplying the national estimate of equipment book value by
the percent of total revenue cars in each region. The omission of locomotives had little impact since regional locomotive percentages followed revenue car percentages very
closely.

1880 to $33,400 in 1890. This evidence supports the con-
tention that price variations within regions over time were
less important than variations among regions at any one
point in time. As an initial correction for this variation
regional dummy variables were introduced in each cross section regression equation.

Summary

The price indexes developed above are indicative of
the problems encountered by the serious student of economic
history. Sources of bias in the estimates may easily be
enumerated, but meaningful corrections require data which
are often unavailable. The year 1888 is a watershed for
statistical data on the railroad sector, and earlier estimates require more careful scrutiny.[22] In this early period
the data on equipment prices are less precise than for
track, and more questionable for cars than locomotives.
The correction for changing capital efficiency by component
was essential to develop reasonable price series for comparable commodities. As expected, the selection of the base
period had a significant impact on the combined track and
equipment index, but fortunately the impact on separate
indexes was far less dramatic. Price variations among

---

[22] Not only did the ICC begin reporting data, but the
quality and coverage of Poor's Manual improved annually and
the Census for 1890 was far more comprehensive than earlier
versions.

regions over time appeared to be less significant than variations among regions at one point in time. Corrections were
made in the formulation of cross section regression equations to account for this variance.

APPENDIX D

GROSS CAPITAL AND INVESTMENT

Introduction

The comparative analysis of investment by a sample of 19 railroad companies and the railroad sector as a whole over the 45 year period from 1870 to 1914 demanded that capital and investment be defined precisely and estimated consistently. This task was complicated by the changes in accounting procedures, capital composition, and capital efficiency over the period. The discussion of capital theory in Chapter III concluded that estimates of gross investment in current dollars and gross capital in constant dollars adjusted for changing efficiency were required for the analysis of the investment decision. The existing annual capital and investment series for the sector in this period were unsatisfactory for this analysis and wide variance in accounting procedures among different firms and over time limited the use of reported financial data, so independent aggregate and company estimates for 1870 to 1914 are derived in this appendix.

In an effort to overcome the deficiencies of the existing data a model was developed to estimate annual capital and investment from changes in the stocks of selected capital components. Annual renewals were derived from a retirement model based on average equipment life. Corrections for changing capital efficiency were applied to equipment stocks and track mileage to derive a series of gross capital in 1910 dollars. Annual price estimates for each component were applied to annual purchases to derive current dollar series of gross investment. The following sections on aggregate data discuss prior capital and investment estimates for the railroad sector in this period, derive series of capital component stocks, develop new capital and investment series and compare the results with the prior estimates. A section on the company estimates discusses the modifications in the aggregate technique required for company data and presents a summary table of sample results.

Prior Aggregate Estimates

The ICC began its reports on annual railroad investment in 1912 and by roughly 1914 the reporting procedures were sufficient to produce reliable estimates.[1] Prior to the Hepburn Act of 1906 accounting procedures were not standardized and no efforts were made to produce annual investment estimates for the sector. The primary index of investment for the period had long been changes in track mileage operated, the only annual physical capital series

---

[1]Melville Ulmer, Capital in Transportation, Communications, and Public Utilities, Op. Cit., pp. 264-5.

which spans the entire period back to 1870, when Melville
Ulmer attempted to improve on the data by exploiting the
wealth of reported financial data.[2]

His method for the period prior to 1912 was to estimate
gross investment for 13 sample years from available Railroad
Commission reports scaled to an aggregate estimate by the
ratio of national to sample book value of road and equipment. Interpolation between those sample years was made by
reference to the series of changes in track mileage. An
adjustment for land purchases produced gross investment
figures. Depreciation was computed as a fixed percentage
of the original cost of road and equipment and subtracted
from gross investment to produce an annual series of net
investment in current dollars. Adjusting for price changes
with a capital input price index produced a constant dollar
series of net investment. ICC data were employed after 1912
and annual net capital stock estimates were derived by
repetitive subtractions of net investment from a 1937 base
of net capital obtained from ICC reports.

Albert Fishlow criticized Ulmer's estimates prior to
1912 on several fronts: (1) the sample estimates overlooked
retirements which were charged to current rather than capital
account, (2) the use of the ratio of book values for scaling
without regard to the age distribution of the sample

---

[2]Ibid.

companies was not appropriate, (3) the interpolating index
was inconsistent with sample estimates, (4) the price index
understated the price decline from 1870 to 1900, particularly in the period from 1880 to 1890.[3] It is clear that
Ulmer's samples were based only on the capital account and,
as Fishlow argues, retirements were charged to current account prior to 1906.[4] Estimates from the retirement model
developed below indicate that this led to an annual under-
statement of gross investment varying from 3% in 1870 to 10%
in 1900. Fishlow's second point is also well taken. Two
of Ulmer's sample State Commission Reports for 1877,
Massachusetts and Kansas,[5] were examined and the level of
gross investment in individual roads was not correlated with
their book values of road and equipment according to an "F"
test at the 90% confidence level. Indeed if all of Ulmer's
state estimates are taken as the sample it is apparent that
there is little correlation of gross investment with book
value.[6]

---

[3]Albert Fishlow, "Productivity and Technological Change
in the Railroad Sector," Op. Cit.

[4]A. M. Sakolski, American Railroad Economics (New York:
The MacMillan Co., 1913), p. 428.

[5]Albert Fishlow, "Productivity and Technological
Change," Op. Cit., p. 591.

[6]Melville Ulmer, Capital in Transportation, Op. Cit.,
p. 266.

The inconsistency of Ulmer's estimates of annual gross investment in sample years with the series of changes in track mileage is perhaps the most serious problem. His investment estimates moved in the opposite direction from his interpolating index in six of his 13 sample years.[7] While the inclusion of equipment in the interpolating index would probably help, road construction remained the principal component of capital formation throughout the period from 1870 to 1914 and the inconsistency probably reflects more on the sample estimates than the interpolating index. Only Fishlow's price index argument is questionable, since Ulmer made two compensating omissions. Ulmer used a questionable "metals and implements" input series, which did not include rail, and assigned it a low weight in his final index.[8] The use of a rail price series with the higher weight suggested in Appendix C would indeed produce a faster decline in the price index, but when allowance is made for changes in rail efficiency over the period the decline is reduced. Table C3 compares a revised price index including rail adjusted for efficiency in column 3 with the Ulmer index adjusted to a 1910 base in column 8. The trends of the series are similar

---

[7]Albert Fishlow, "Productivity and Technological Change," Op. Cit., p. 593.

[8]Wholesale Prices, Wages and Transportation, Senate Report No. 1394, Part I, as cited by Melville Ulmer, Capital in Transportation, Op. Cit., p. 277.

although there is considerable variance in annual estimates. Fishlow's price index criticism was justified, but while annual estimates are affected it is doubtful that Ulmer's price index produced any major distortion of the trend of investment.

It is clear, however, that Ulmer's annual series of net capital and investment may no longer be used with confidence. Fishlow produced alternate decadal estimates of net capital in 1910 dollars for the period from 1840 to 1910 based on track mileage and stocks of passenger cars. Changes in the net capital stock were determined by estimating decadal purchases corrected for retirements, subtracting depreciation, and weighting components by an estimate of their 1910 reproduction cost.

> The principle involved is clear. Each physical unit, whether of track or equipment, should be weighted by its cost of reproduction in the prices and technology of a given year before being compared. In this way one gets a consistent measure of the capital stock over time, where real investment is measured, as is conventional, by its cost, not its capacity.[9]

Fishlow estimated reproduction costs in 1910 based on relative equipment and track weights and the percentage of cost variance associated with weight changes.

Unfortunately, in the investment decision the relevant capital variable is capacity rather than cost. Thus, while

[9]Albert Fishlow, "Productivity and Technological Changes," Op. Cit., p. 595.

many of Fishlow's estimates were helpful, some way of adjusting component purchases for changing efficiency rather than 1910 reproduction costs was required. It must be noted that Fishlow did not overlook efficiency changes but merely isolated them for separate analysis.

An additional study of investment in the railroad sector from 1897 to 1914 by Larry Neal became available while this paper was in progress.[10] His technique was to scale gross investment reported by a sample of 21 territorially distributed companies to a national estimate by the ratio of national to sample miles operated. An estimate of annual renewals charged to operating expenses was added to derive national gross investment. Depreciation rates were selected to develop net capital stock estimates which were consistent with Fishlow's decadal estimates. Neal checked his results against independent estimates of equipment production and extended the results to 1915 for comparison with ICC data. Neither comparison provided strong support but both were roughly consistent with his estimates. His capital price index, shown in column 7 of Table C3, does not adjust for changing efficiency but is comparable with the index derived in column 3. Neal made his company worksheets available and the estimates were carefully derived. His results were used

---

[10]Larry Neal, "Investment Behavior by American Railroads, 1897-1914," Op. Cit.

to test the validity of the investment estimates derived below for 1897 to 1914.

Annual Sector Track and Equipment Estimates

Annual estimates of locomotives, passenger cars, and freight cars as well as main and "other" track mileage were required to compute annual capital and investment series. Annual estimates of locomotives, freight cars, and passenger cars in operation were reported by Poor's Manual of the Railroads beginning in 1876[11] and by the ICC after 1890.[12] The passenger car data includes estimates of baggage and mail cars. Poor estimated annual main track mileage back to 1830, but his series of main and other track dates from 1876.[13] ICC track data begin in 1890.[14] To complete the record back to 1870 equipment estimates were derived from a nineteen road sample for 1870 to 1876, ICC and Poor data were linked, and other track estimates were produced for 1870 to 1876.

---

[11]Henry Poor, Manual of the Railroads, as cited in Bureau of Census, Historical Statistics, Op. Cit., Series Q 18, 20, 21, p. 427.

[12]ICC, Statistics of Railways in the United States, as cited by Bureau of Census, Historical Statistics, Op. Cit., Series Q 55, p. 429, Series Q 61, 64, p. 430.

[13]Henry Poor, Manual of the Railroads, as cited in Bureau of Census, Historical Statistics, Op. Cit., Series Q 15, 17, p. 427.

[14]ICC, Statistics of Railways in the United States, as cited in Bureau of Census, Historical Statistics, Op. Cit., Series Q 48, 49, p. 429.

Equipment sums from a 19 road sample were scaled to annual aggregate estimates by the ratio of national to sample gross earnings and used to interpolate between Fishlow's 1869[15] and Poor's 1876 equipment figures. The use of the earnings scaling technique was checked by comparing the scaled equipment estimates for 1870, 1877 and 1880 with alternate figures shown in Table D1. The freight car estimates were consistently low as was the 1880 passenger car figure. The alternate locomotive and passenger car estimates for 1870 and 1877 were reasonably consistent, however, and the trend of the scaled equipment estimates used in interpolation was consistent with the trend of alternate estimates in every case. The interpolation technique was checked by comparing the estimates for June 1873 from Table D2 with figures from the Railway Monitor for December 1873 of 14,223 locomotives, 13,574 passenger cars, and 338,427 freight cars.[16] The estimates varied by 8.5% for passenger cars, 3.6% for locomotives, and 1.3% for freight cars, and generally support the interpolation procedure.

Poor's locomotive estimate for 1890 was simply averaged with the ICC estimate to link the two series since the estimates were comparable. The ICC passenger car and freight

---

[15]Albert Fishlow, "Productivity and Technological Changes," Op. Cit., p. 602.

[16]The Railway Monitor (December 31, 1873), p. 376.

Table D1

EQUIPMENT STOCK ESTIMATES 1870, 1877, 1880

Year	1	2	3	4
		Locomotives		
1870	9,930	10,000		
1877	16,592		15,911	
1880	17,470		17,949	17,391
		Passenger Cars		
1870	9,700	10,000		
1877	14,096		15,907	
1880	14,681		17,544	16,176
		Freight Cars		
1870	169,189	185,000		
1877	352,237		392,175	
1880	458,621		539,255	499,442

Column	Description
1	Fifteen company sample scaled by the ratio of national to sample gross earnings as of June 30.
2	Estimate from Albert Fishlow, "Productivity and Technological Change," Op. Cit, p. 602. Figures are for December 31, 1869.
3	Poor's Manual of the Railroads as cited by the Bureau of the Census, Historical Statistics, Series Q18, Q20, Q21, p. 427. Data are for June 30.
4	Bureau of the Census, Tenth Census of the United States, 1880, Vol. IV, Transportation (Washington, D.C.: 1880). Data are for June 30.

car estimates were substantially lower than Poor's 1890 figures due to the incomplete initial ICC reports. To compensate for this change in coverage ICC car estimates were increased by the ratio of Poor to ICC data in 1890, 1.16 for freight cars and 1.08 for passenger cars. The correction factor was linearly reduced to 1.0 in 1900 as ICC coverage increased. The final equipment estimates are presented in Table D2. The track adjustment for the transition from Poor to ICC data was accomplished by averaging the 1890 figures. Annual estimates of the ratio of other to main track for 1870 to 1876 were derived by linear interpolation between Fishlow's 1869 estimate of .20[17] and the average ratio of other to main track from 1877 to 1890, .24. Multiplying the annual estimated ratio by main track produced other track mileage figures. The final annual track figures are also shown in Table D2.

Annual equipment estimates for 1845 to 1870 for passenger cars and 1850 to 1870 for freight cars were also required to derive annual retirement estimates. Annual purchases in this period were derived by interpolating between Fishlow's decadal estimates[18] with respect to his series of annual net

---

[17]Albert Fishlow, "Productivity and Technological Changes," Op. Cit., p. 596.

[18]Ibid., p. 602.

Table D2

ANNUAL EQUIPMENT STOCK AND TRACK MILEAGE ESTIMATES 1870-1914[a]

Fiscal Year	Locomotives	Passenger Cars	Freight Cars	Main Track	Other Track
1870	10,276	10,451	201,220	49,833	9,967
1871	11,348	11,321	216,825	56,612	11,889
1872	12,475	11,366	269,100	63,236	13,280
1873	14,750	12,515	343,900	68,220	15,003
1874	15,250	13,138	369,200	72,327	15,119
1875	15,260	13,421	378,800	73,241	16,845
1876	15,618	14,621	384,903	75,452	17,354
1877	15,911	15,907	392,175	77,945	18,042
1878	16,445	16,096	423,013	80,415	20,064
1879	17,084	16,528	480,190	84,152	20,051
1880	17,949	17,575	539,255	89,909	20,293
1881	19,911	18,923	648,295	98,185	24,866
1882	21,889	20,498	730,435	108,893	26,774
1883	23,405	22,078	778,663	118,050	26,890
1884	24,353	22,555	798,399	123,384	29,374
1885	25,662	22,541	805,517	126,883	31,577
1886	26,108	24,690	845,912	132,329	31,900
1887	27,275	25,893	950,889	142,776	33,668
1888	29,006	27,074	1,005,108	152,664	35,492
1889	30,566	28,524	1,051,141	158,695	38,037
1890	30,976	28,917	1,061,952	160,197	42,301
1891	32,139	30,185	1,098,868	161,275	46,170
1892	33,136	30,897	1,102,367	162,397	48,654
1893	34,788	33,267	1,134,904	169,780	52,084
1894	35,492	34,669	1,325,686	175,691	54,104
1895	35,699	34,768	1,303,770	177,746	55,529
1896	35,950	34,323	1,319,638	181,983	57,158
1897	35,986	34,635	1,275,034	183,284	58,729
1898	36,234	34,267	1,298,779	184,648	60,685
1899	36,703	34,289	1,321,420	187,535	62,608

Table D2 (Continued)

Fiscal Year	Locomotives	Passenger Cars	Freight Cars	Main Track	Other Track
1900	37,663	34,713	1,365,531	192,556	66,228
1901	39,584	35,969	1,464,328	195,562	69,791
1902	41,225	36,987	1,546,101	200,155	74,041
1903	43,871	38,140	1,653,782	205,314	78,508
1904	46,743	39,752	1,692,194	212,243	84,830
1905	48,357	40,713	1,731,409	216,974	89,823
1906	51,672	42,262	1,837,914	222,340	94,743
1907	55,388	43,973	1,991,557	227,455	100,520
1908	57,698	45,292	2,100,784	230,494	103,152
1909	58,219	45,664	2,086,835	235,402	106,950
1910	60,019	47,179	2,148,478	240,831	110,936
1911	62,463	49,906	2,208,997	246,238	116,587
1912	63,463	51,583	2,229,163	249,852	121,386
1913	65,597	52,717	2,298,478	253,470	126,038
1914	67,012	54,492	2,349,734	256,547	130,661

[a]The derivation of each equipment stock and track mileage series is discussed in detail in the text.

investment from 1845 to 1859[19] and with respect to changes
in main track mileage from 1859 to 1870.

The Capital and Investment Model

Investment and capital estimates were limited to the
four principal components cited above: (1) track, (2) locomotives, (3) passenger cars, (4) freight cars. Annual gross
investment was computed as the sum of annual expenditures on
each of those components. No corrections were made for
changing component efficiency since actual "out of pocket"
expenditures for capital goods were desired. Annual component purchases were computed as the change in the component
stock plus renewals minus retirements, or since no efficiency
or depreciation adjustments were made, simply changes in
component stocks. Annual equipment prices were taken from
Table C5 and annual main track prices were computed by multiplying the 1910 cost of main track per mile, $40,200,[20]
times the track price index in column 1 of Table F1. The
cost of all other track including sidings and yard track was
taken as one-half the cost of main track.[21] Annual series
of track mileage and numbers of locomotives, passenger cars,

---

[19] Albert Fishlow, American Railroads and the Transformation of the Ante-Bellum Economy (Cambridge: Harvard University Press, 1965), p. 399.

[20] Albert Fishlow, "Productivity and Technological
Changes," Op. Cit., p. 608.

[21] Ibid, pp. 597-598.

and freight cars were derived in the last section. Applying
annual prices to the first differences in those series produced aggregate series of gross investment in track and
equipment, track, and equipment in current dollars as shown
in columns 1, 2, and 3 respectively of Table F1.

The capital model is more complicated since it adjusts
annual additions by the relative efficiency of the capital
component. The capital stock at any time is the sum of sur-
viving additions, where each addition is weighted by the
capital efficiency index for its vintage. Since different
efficiency adjustments are required for the retirement of
old vintages and their corresponding new vintage renewals, a
retirement model is required. Fishlow estimated retirements
based on equipment lives of twenty years for locomotives
and freight cars and twenty-five years for passenger cars.[22]
Those estimates were checked against the records of purchases and retirements of the South Carolina Railroad,[23] and
the Burlington Railroad,[24] as well as the estimates reported

---

[22]Ibid, p. 601.

[23]Samuel Derrick, Centennial History of the South
Carolina Railroad (Columbia: The State Co., 1930) Appendix
VI, pp. 314-321.

[24]Bernard Corbin and William Kerka, Steam Locomotives
of the Burlington Route (Red Oak, Iowa: Thomas M. Murphy
Co., 1960), pp. 256-263.

by Wellington,[25] and found to be generally typical. The
scarcity of retirement data prevented the creation of a more
detailed retirement scheme based on survival curves or the
impact of the business cycle on the timing of retirements.
It is clear that retirements tended to be concentrated during
the upswing of the cycle so that the use of a fixed equipment
life to derive retirements may lead to some annual distortion.[26]

The efficiency index for each capital component derived
in Appendix E was then applied to all purchases to obtain
an estimate of 1910 efficiency equivalent purchases. The
appropriate index for the vintage of retirements was applied
to obtain an estimate of 1910 efficiency equivalent retirements. The difference of corrected purchases and retirements
produced the estimate of efficiency adjusted gross additions
for each component. Multiplication of each component by
its 1910 price and summation over all components produced
annual estimates of the gross capital stock in 1910 dollars.
The resulting capital series for track and equipment,

---

[25]A. M. Wellington, The Economic Theory of the Location
of Railways (6th ed rev; New York: John Wiley and Sons,
1906), pp. 418-419.

[26]Larry Neal, "Investment Behavior by American Railroads, 1897-1914," Op. Cit., p. 131. Thomas Woodcock,
Anatomy of a Railroad Report (New York: U.S. Book Co.,
1895), p. 15.

equipment, and track are shown in columns 4, 5, and 6 respectively of Table F1.

The interpretation of the capital and investment series
derived above is straightforward. The capital stock measures
the capacity of the track and equipment in place in terms
of 1910 efficiency units, assuming that the contribution of
each component to production does not vary over its average
life. The investment series measures the expenditures in
current dollars represented by annual additions to the
capital stock, where additions are measured by equipment
deliveries or track completed rather than orders or track
starts. Comparison of the investment series with alternate
series based on payments for capital goods rather than deliveries must account for any lag between charges to the
capital account of reporting companies and the addition of
the physical good to the capital stock.

The available evidence on such lags is mixed since companies varied in the timing of charges to capital account.
Equipment expenditures and additions cause little concern
with annual data, but track projects often lasted several
years. Road surveys were generally completed and construction underway prior to financing and subsequent expenditures,[27] but the process of charges during construction must

---

[27]A. M. Wellington, The Economic Theory of the Location
of Railways, Op. Cit., pp. 418-419.

be examined. Track projects were habitually laid out in
annual segments to take advantage of weather conditions and
expedite use of completed segments. The Railway Gazette
observed in 1873 that:

> Nearly two-thirds of track laying is usually done
> in the last five months of the year . . . largely
> because a great deal of grading is usually done
> earlier, so that a large amount of road bed is
> ready for the rails.[28]

As a result most roads reported annual track completions,
even on projects which were still underway. Some expenditures listed on annual reports did correspond to future road
completions, but in most cases annual expenditures corresponded to annual completions.[29] Indeed some roads waited
until projects were completed to charge all expenditures to
capital account,[30] but those cases are balanced by other
roads which reported sizeable construction advances.[31] It
is difficult to weigh the evidence since contradictory ex-
amples may always be found and the crucial question centers
on the accounting procedures used on a majority of roads.

---

[28]Railroad Gazette, Vol. III, p. 321.

[29]For example, the Annual Report of the Northern Pacific Railroad for 1897 to 1914 listed road completed and
corresponding expenditures.

[30]For example, the Annual Report of the Boston and
Maine Railroad, June 30, 1900, listed expenditures of
$387,736 for 16.5 miles of road begun in 1898.

[31]For example, the Annual Report of the Chicago, Rock
Island and Pacific Railroad, June 30, 1903, listed large
construction advances.

For the nineteen company sample used throughout this analysis, however, the accounts suggest that annual charges to
capital account correspond to additions in that reporting
period so that annual expenditure and completion data should
be comparable.

Comparison of Sector Capital and Investment Estimates

The gross capital and investment series may be compared
with alternate estimates to investigate the validity of their
trends and annual variation. Both series apply only to track,
locomotives, passenger cars, and freight cars. Fishlow
estimated that these components accounted for 85% of total
investment in the 1850s[32] and ICC figures suggest a coverage
of 75% by 1918.[33] An analysis of railroad commission reports from three states in the periods 1874-1876, 1885-1887,
and 1896-1898 suggested steady reductions in coverage of
83, 77, and 76 per cent respectively.[34] The period from
1875 to 1886 apparently brought a marked increase in the
substitution of alternate capital goods such as electrification,

---

[32]Albert Fishlow, "Productivity and Technological
Changes," Op. Cit., pp. 594-595.

[33]ICC, Statistics of Railways in the United States for
1918, as cited by Albert Fishlow, "Productivity and Technological Changes," Op. Cit., p. 595.

[34]For 1874-1876 and 1896-1898 New York, Massachusetts
and Michigan reports were used and for 1885-1887 Massachusetts, Michigan and the Dakotas. The samples included
roughly 25 companies reporting the desired data annually.

buildings, and track straightening. The capital and investment series thus represent a high, albeit decreasing, percentage of total capital and investment.

Alternate decadal capital stock estimates are presented
in Table D3. The estimate of gross capital stock shown in
column 2 was derived by using Fishlow's technique of estimating 1910 reproduction costs from changing component
weights.[35] Annual component weights were derived by linear
interpolation of the semi-decadal estimates shown in Table
D4. Annual purchases and retirements were derived as discussed above for the efficiency adjusted capital series.
The efficiency of capital components, discussed in Appendix
E, increased more rapidly than Fishlow's reproduction cost
series leading to the variance between columns 1 and 2 in
Table D3. The net capital series in column 3 was derived
by applying Fishlow's depreciation rates to column 2. The
use of annual data led to the minor differences between that
series and the one derived by Fishlow in column 6. Ulmer's
net capital estimates are presented in column 4 and Neal's
in column 5.

The close correspondence of all the net estimates for
1909 with the efficiency adjusted gross series in column 1
of Table D3 is striking. The net series were forced to

---

[35]Albert Fishlow, "Productivity and Technological
Changes,", Op. Cit., especially pp. 596, 602, 604, 605.

Table D3

CAPITAL STOCK ESTIMATES (Millions 1910 Dollars)

Year	1	2	3	4	5	6
1870	1173	2015	1761	3910		1741
1879	1971	3817	3335	5780		3297
1889	4583	7692	6550	7750		6474
1899	6400	9768	7650	8600	7795	7560
1909	10596	13810	10580	10460	10957	10458

Column	Description
Year	Data are for June 30 of the year cited. The figure listed for 1870 in column 1 is for 1871. Columns 3, 4, and 6 for 1870 are 1869 data.
1	My gross capital stock accounting for efficiency changes and estimating replacements from average equipment lives.
2	Gross capital stock computed by Albert Fishlow's technique in "Productivity and Technological Change," Op. Cit, for obtaining 1910 production costs, but based on annual track and equipment estimates.
3	Net capital stock computed by applying Fishlow's depreciation rates to gross capital in column 2.
4	Net capital stock computed by Melville Ulmer, Capital in Transportation, Communications and Public Utilities, Op. Cit., pp. 256-7. Annual data were averaged to obtain June 30 figures.
5	Net capital stock from Larry Neal, "Investment Behavior by American Railroads," Op. Cit., p. 132.
6	Net capital stock computed by Albert Fishlow, "Productivity and Technological Change," Op. Cit., p. 606.

Table D4

CAPITAL COMPONENT WEIGHT ESTIMATES 1870-1910[a]

Fiscal Year	Locomotives (Tons)	Freight Cars (Tons)	Passenger Cars (Tons)	Track (Tons/Mile)
1870	32.5	10.5	18.0	85.0
1875	35.0	11.0	20.0	87.5
1880	40.0	11.8	23.5	90.0
1885	45.0	12.5	27.0	95.0
1890	51.5	14.1	31.0	100.0
1895	58.0	15.7	35.0	103.8
1900	68.0	17.0	40.0	107.5
1905	78.0	18.3	45.0	111.8
1910	72.0	17.5	39.0	115.0

[a]Equipment weights were derived from Albert Fishlow's estimates in "Productivity and Technological Change," Op. Cit., p. 604. The weights for his ten year periods were used for the center year of the period, while the averages of adjoining decades were used for end years. Decadal track weights are from the same article, p. 596, and semi-decadal estimates were derived by linear interpolation.

converge with Ulmer's estimates by derivation, but the gross series derived from sums of purchases and retirements is not linked to any alternate estimate. The efficiency adjusted series falls off rapidly, however, and by 1870 it is far below the alternate estimates. Ulmer's net estimates are obviously much higher than any alternate net series, and are even higher than all gross estimates before 1890. The efficiency adjusted gross capital series thus deviates from the alternate series in the expected directions and converges with alternate net capital series in 1910.

The gross investment estimates in current dollars also represent a large but decreasing percentage of total investment. Figure D1 compares the road and equipment series with the Neal[36] and Ulmer[37] figures for 1896-1914. The similarity of the investment series with Neal's estimates is striking. The road and equipment series closely follows Neal's annual variations and remains at roughly 75% of his estimates. Since the road and equipment series is based on annual physical additions and Neal's series is based on annual expenditures, the close fit of the two series suggests that no lead of reported outlays over reported additions is required. Ulmer's series, on the other hand, shows

---

[36]Larry Neal, "Investment Behavior by American Railroads, 1897-1914," Op. Cit., p. 131.

[37]Melville Ulmer, Capital in Transportation, Op. Cit., pp. 256-257.

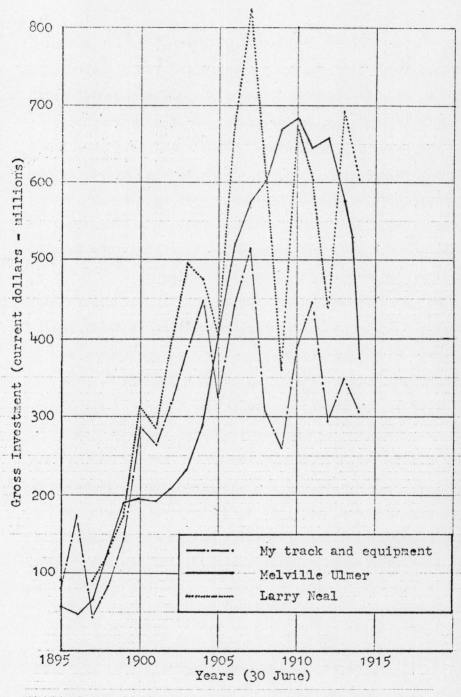

Fig. D1. ‒ ‒ Graph of annual gross investment estimates, 1895-1914

little annual variation and is not affected by the recessions of 1904-5 or 1907-8. The Ulmer series also shows a maximum investment in 1910 due to his sample estimate for that year,[38] while the other series reach their highest peaks in 1906-7.

The Ulmer and road and equipment investment series are compared from 1870 to 1914 in Table D5, and the figures are portrayed graphically in Figure D2. Ulmer's series diverges from the physical estimates in the late 1880s and early 1890s, possibly due to his high sample estimates for 1891 and 1892,[39] and surprisingly remains below the physical estimates which should constitute roughly 75 to 80 percent of Ulmer's total investment figures. Ulmer's estimates continue to show less annual variation than the physical series prior to 1895.

The comparison of the physical investment series with Neal's estimates suggest that the physical series correctly follows the annual variation and trend of total investment. The divergence of the results from Ulmer's estimates suggest that Ulmer's annual variation is questionable and that his estimates prior to 1895 understate total investment.

---

[38] Ibid, p. 266.

[39] Ibid.

Table D5

ALTERNATE ESTIMATES OF GROSS INVESTMENT 1870-1914

(Millions of Current Dollars)

Year	1	2	Year	1	2	3
1870		400	1893	354	312	
1871		399	1894	328	129	
1872	545	320	1895	80	58	
1873	464	205	1896	174	48	
1874	258	127	1897	42	65	90
1875	96	104	1898	82	129	128
1876	126	110	1899	146	190	172
1877	124	116	1900	287	196	313
1878	150	119	1901	264	193	287
1879	183	204	1902	318	209	400
1880	314	361	1903	386	233	497
1881	551	419	1904	446	289	475
1882	556	340	1905	326	402	406
1883	394	241	1906	444	522	671
1884	249	175	1907	514	573	824
1885	173	178	1908	308	601	601
1886	237	241	1909	260	670	360
1887	487	263	1910	385	684	672
1888	418	239	1911	443	645	602
1889	291	229	1912	293	659	439
1890	162	234	1913	349	574	693
1891	114	322	1914	306	373	604
1892	101	420				

Column	Description
Year	All data are for June 30 of the year listed.
1	My estimate of annual investment derived from annual purchases of track and equipment multiplied by component prices.
2	Melville Ulmer, Capital in Transportation, Communications and Public Utilities, Op. Cit., pp. 256-257. Annual figures averaged to June 30.
3	Larry Neal, "Investment Behavior by American Railroads," Op. Cit., p. 132.

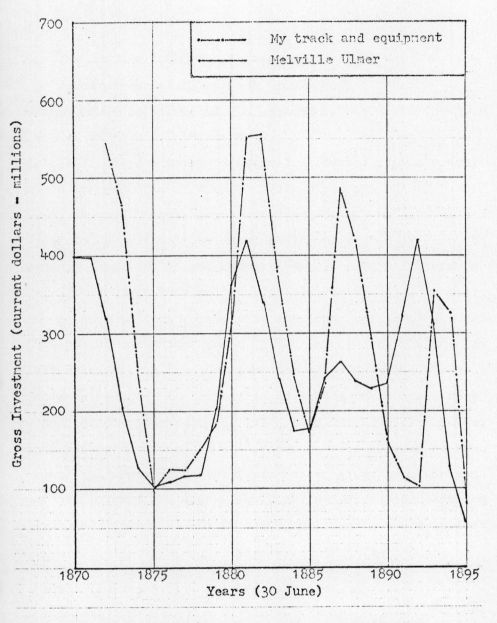

Fig. D2. - - Graph of annual gross investment
estimates, 1870-1895

Company Capital and Investment Estimates

A wealth of information is reported at the company level which is not available for the sector as a whole. However, detailed information on the composition and magnitude of gross investment was not uniformly reported and is difficult to interpret. Perhaps Woodcock's brief analysis best explains the difficulty. "There is probably not a single road in the country whose construction account does not contain a vast amount of items representing absolutely no value."[40] With limited supervision of railroad accounts prior to 1906, despite the best efforts of Henry Poor, charges to various accounts were often based as much on whim as accounting procedure. Since most roads operated on the premise that investors wanted earnings to go to dividends and new investment to be financed by bonds, investment was often overstated to justify new debt which could then be used to meet dividend payment.[41] Construction and earnings accounts could be adjusted simply by overcharges for transportation costs in construction. Where the owners also controlled the construction companies the inducement to over-

---

[40]Thomas Woodcock, Anatomy of a Railroad Report, Op. Cit., p. 23.

[41]Arthur Hadley, Railroad Transportation, Its History and Laws (New York: G. P. Putnam's Sons, 1899), pp. 56-62.

charges for other construction costs were numerous.[42] Out-
standing credits, rather than actual construction expenditures, were commonly regarded as the measure of the book
cost of property.[43]

These factors make the accuracy and consistency of the
reported financial data questionable. If the analysis were
limited to individual companies over time an argument could
be made that the data contained a consistent bias and
accurately reflected annual variations. But where cross-
section analysis is desired consistency of the data over all
firms is essential. Fortunately the technique of deriving
capital and investment estimates from the principal physical capital components used in the aggregate series can be
employed for individual companies as well. Physical series
were widely and uniformly reported over the period so it
was possible to select companies for analysis which did not
report financial capital accounts in detail. There was
little reason for companies to distort the series of physical components and Adams noted that, "railroad accountants

---

[42]William Ripley, Railroads: Finance and Organization
(New York: Longman's, Green and Co., 1915), pp. 1-83,
227-280.

[43]Henry Adams, American Railway Accounting (New York:
Henry Holt and Co., 1913), p. 47.

are very profuse in this sort of information as a rule, as
it 'gives away' very little."[44]

The technique outlined in detail for the aggregate
gross capital series in constant dollars and gross investment series in current dollars was applied to data for 19
sample firms to produce annual individual company series for
1870 to 1914. Retirements were estimated from average equipment lives as before, but purchases prior to 1870 were determined by linear interpolation between decadal equipment
estimates for each company. Table D6 summarizes the resultant annual series by presenting decadal capital stock
estimates in 1910 dollars for each company.

Summary

The results of this analysis are new aggregate series
of gross capital in 1910 dollars and gross investment in
current dollars from 1872 to 1914, and corresponding estimates for 19 sample companies from 1870 to 1914. The derivations are based on the application of efficiency adjustments for capital and current prices for investment to
estimated annual equipment and track purchases. The capital
series present a new technique of applying efficiency adjustments directly to stock estimates in an effort to
accurately measure the capacity of capital to contribute to

---

[44]Ibid, pp. 34-35.

Table D6

COMPANY GROSS CAPITAL STOCK ESTIMATES (Millions 1910 Dollars)

Company[a]	Fiscal Year				
	1871	1880	1890	1900	1910
1	3.19	5.56	26.42	45.88	75.54
2	2.86	7.17	9.83	14.25	22.43
3	4.02	6.74	21.92	105.83	136.10
4	21.36	43.29	73.32	125.83	246.33
5	29.00	45.39	76.32	169.88	280.36
6	25.84	34.54	56.24	111.87	141.49
7	53.17	87.55	132.37	244.93	429.83
8	6.01	15.56	35.68	47.30	73.13
9	22.62	64.16	130.48	205.07	365.60
10	14.61	58.55	150.95	277.16	376.77
11	21.99	91.75	160.45	215.28	289.54
12	16.52	28.41	92.78	151.33	236.56
13	8.35	23.07	57.47	71.22	85.56
14	8.19	35.09	55.68	102.79	179.51
15	10.80	11.05	18.70	29.24	47.89
16	20.71	26.86	56.59	103.41	168.91
17	1.25	33.93	150.06	171.53	372.33
18	0.00	24.04	68.76	182.60	291.67
19	6.68	13.05	51.34	101.32	202.38
Total	276.87	646.19	1423.36	2476.72	4021.93
U.S. Total[b]	1334.	2143.	4732.	6743.	10995.
Sample % of U.S. Total	21	30	30	37	37

[a]The company numerical code is explained in Table G1.

[b]Gross capital stock estimates for the entire sector are taken from column 4 of Table F1. The estimate listed for 1871 is for 1872.

current production. The gross investment estimates simply measure annual expenditures for new track and equipment and constitute roughly 75 to 80 percent of total investment over the period. The physical component approach made it possible to develop consistent capital and investment estimates for 19 companies over a 45 year period, reducing the variance of the estimates from heterogeneous financial reporting procedures. The company estimates are consistent with those produced for the entire sector, simplifying the comparative analysis of the investment decision at the company and sector levels.

APPENDIX E

MEASURES OF CAPITAL COMPONENT PERFORMANCE

Introduction

In order to estimate the changing capacity of the capital stock over time the assortment of relevant capital goods
must be reduced to a manageable set of comparable commodities.
This comparability is often assumed in the statistical estimation of production relationships, and incomparability is
just as often cited as a principal cause of the large resulting unexplained residual. Where many capital goods must
be compared with respect to the quality of output, capacity,
and cost of operation, it is understandable that few capital
series have been developed which deal explicitly with technical change. Yet the railroad sector from 1870 to 1914
was characterized by a rapid rate of technical change and an
investment study of the period would be incomplete without
an analysis of that change. Fortunately, four capital goods
accounted for roughly seventy-five percent of all railroad
investment in the period, so that it is feasible to limit
analysis to those four capital goods.[1] In addition the

---

[1]Albert Fishlow, "Productivity," Op. Cit., p. 594.

243

record of technical change for each component is well documented so that meaningful measures of relative performance may be derived.

The period from 1870 to 1914 produced dramatic changes in railroad technology. The adoption of steel rail in place of iron with accompanying improvements in road bed dramatically increased the load bearing capacity of track. Improvements in locomotive design brought a tripling in tractive power while engine weight doubled. Freight car capacity also tripled over the period while passenger car capacity steadily increased. The economic impact of rolling stock improvements was significant since operating costs per train-mile increased slowly with expanded locomotive weight,[2] increases in car capacity were obtained with small additions to dead weight, and coal consumption increased very little with increases in car weight.[3] Improvements in signals, brakes, and couplers had significant impacts on safety, but were of limited economic significance.[4]

Indices of the changing level of performance of each of the principal components of capital, track, locomotives, freight cars, and passenger cars, were developed for use in

---

[2]A. M. Wellington, Location of the Railways, Op. Cit., p. 567.

[3]Ibid.

[4]Albert Fishlow, "Productivity," Op. Cit., pp. 636-639.

the analysis of investment behavior. Each index was designed to trace the most economically significant changes in the component based on physical characteristics rather than techniques of employment. Durability distinctions were not considered since the touchstone of comparison was current contribution to production. Differences in durability affect depreciation, and hence value, but they do not affect the contribution to current output.[5] The index for each component was based on an index of capacity divided by an index of the cost of operation.

Track

The capacity of rail may be traced by examining the weight of new equipment employed in any given year. Where safety margins were essential, rolling stock weights measure the useable capacity of rail. In addition, improvements in track capacity could be exploited only by subsequent improvements in rolling stock with some time lag. Locomotive weight accounted for most track wear and represented the largest point load on the track.[6] Therefore the average weight of new locomotives was employed as the measure of track capacity. Since no correction for changing operating

---

[5]Trygve Haavelmo, A Study in the Theory of Investment, Op. Cit., p. 82.

[6]A. M. Wellington, Location of the Railways, Op. Cit., p. 122.

cost was required for track, the final performance index is merely the ratio of the weight of new locomotives in a given year to the weight in 1910, as shown in column 1 of Table E2.

Some engineering studies are available to check the results obtained by using locomotive weight as the measure of rail capacity. Any such comparison is complicated by the shift from iron to steel rail during the first half of the period from 1870 to 1914. In steel rail the stiffness, or resistance to bending, increases as the square of the rail weight. Strength, or the capacity to bear weight without crushing, varies with rail weight to the 1.5 power.[7] The capacity to resist crushing was of dominant importance in accomodating rapid weight increases in rolling stock. Table E1 shown below compares the indices of rail stiffness and strength based on steel engineering data with the locomotive weight capacity index.

---

[7]Ibid.

Table E1

MEASURES OF RAIL CAPACITY 1910 = 100

Year	Engineering Strength	Engineering Stiffness	Locomotive[a] Weight
1870	43	32	45
1880	46	36	56
1890	56	46	72
1900	78	72	95
1910	100	100	100

[a]Locomotive weights are listed in Table D4.

For purposes of comparison the engineering data for 1870 and 1880 should be reduced to account for the proportionate use of iron rail in those periods. If this is done the engineering strength index consistently understates the locomotive index by roughly twenty percent prior to 1910. In other words the engineering data suggest that rail capacity increased more rapidly than locomotive weight, but that the difference in trend was quite uniform. This divergence is in the expected direction due to the safety margins and new equipment time lags cited above. In general the engineering evidence is quite consistent with the trend and magnitudes suggested by the locomotive weight capacity index.

Locomotives

The power developed by a locomotive and transmitted to the train in terms of pulling capacity is the result of boiler, transmission, and tractive power. Boiler power is generally limited by the safe quantity of steam which can be produced, and tractive power is limited by the proportion of the locomotive's weight which can be effectively placed on the driving wheels. Transmission of the power generated by the rapidly expanding steam to the driving wheels requires a conversion to mechanical energy in the cylinder. The cylinder can be adapted to transmit any reasonable amount of power in the desired ratio of speed and force by minor modifications in weight at relatively small cost.[3]

Boiler power may be expanded with substantial increases in weight within the limits of admissible load per wheel. Wellington estimated that a ten percent increase in engine boiler power required an increase in engine weight of eight percent.[9] Tractive power is determined by the weight of the engine, the weight distribution, the number and location of the driving wheels, the adhesion of the driving wheels on the track, and boiler power. Tractive power is necessarily limited by the strength of rail and road structure. In general, with a given boiler a ten percent increase in tractive power required a forty percent increase in the load on the drivers or a fifty percent increase in

---

[8]Ibid, p. 400.

[9]Ibid, p. 402.

total engine weight.[10] This discussion suggests that expanded locomotive power was closely linked to improvements in track.[11]

Potential tractive power reflects the limitation on the conversion of boiler power to static pulling force in a particular locomotive. Since boiler power may be divided between tractive power and speed up to the limitations of the cylinder, an upper bound to tractive power produces a lower bound to operating speed. Within the design restrictions imposed by maximum tractive power, variations in boiler power produce variations in operating speed. Increases in speed were of limited economic importance, and average freight and passenger train speeds remained constant from 1890 to 1910.[12] This suggests that tractive power was the central variable in locomotive performance and partially explains the dramatic design changes over the period to increase the weight on the drivers and the number of drivers.[13]

The locomotive capacity index therefore reflects changes in tractive power. A principal feature of improvements in

---

[10]Ibid, pp. 402, 438-441.

[11]This is consistent with the conclusion reached by Albert Fishlow, "Productivity," Op. Cit., p. 640.

[12]Ibid, p. 637.

[13]Jacob Schmookler, Invention and Economic Growth (Cambridge, Mass.: Harvard University Press, 1966), pp. 276-7.

locomotive design over the period was an increase in the
ratio of tractive power to engine weight. The relationship
of locomotive weight to tractive power over the period from
1870 to 1914 is shown on Figure E1.[14] Tractive power for
selected years was derived from the graph by using a representative locomotive model and weight for those years. An
annual index of capacity was completed by linear interpolation between those years.

The increased weight which enabled dramatic increases
in tractive power also produced increases in operating costs
per locomotive. Wellington estimated that a doubling of the
weight of a locomotive hauling a given train would increase
the operating costs by 14.1 percent.[15] Based on this estimate the operating costs per locomotive in any given year
relative to the operating cost in 1910 were estimated. This
operating cost index was divided into the tractive power

---

[14]A. M. Wellington, Location of the Railways, Op. Cit.,
pp. 438-440. Edwin P. Alexander, American Locomotives (New
York: W. W. Norton and Co., Inc., 1950), pp. 22, 44-52, 76-
80. George L. Fowler (ed), Forney's Catechism of the Locomotive, Part I, (3rd rev ed, New York: The Railway Age
Gazette, 1911), p. 89. Paul T. Warner, Locomotives of the
Pennsylvania Railroad, 1834-1924, (Chicago: Owen Davies,
1959), pp. 28, 35, 42, 46. American Locomotive Company, Exhibit of the American Locomotive Company (New York: American
Locomotive Company, 1904), pp. 31, 33, 35. Observations shown
on the graph are summarized by a single straight line for each
model regardless of the source of information.

[15]A. M. Wellington, Location of the Railways, Op. Cit.,
p. 567.

251

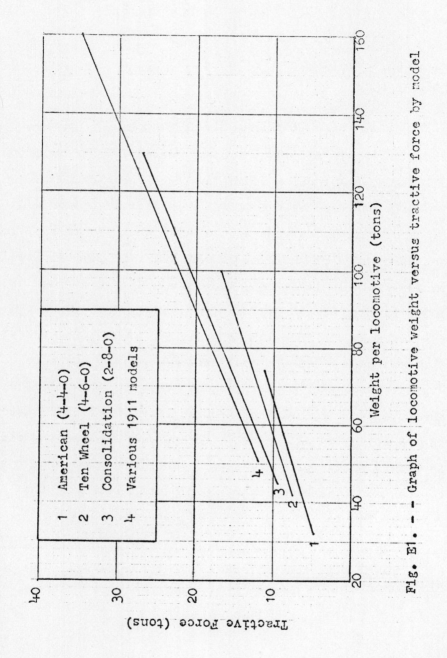

Fig. E1. -- Graph of locomotive weight versus tractive force by model

capacity index to produce the locomotive performance index, as shown in column 4 of Table E2.

Freight Cars

The capacity of freight cars at different periods is reasonably well recorded, but the variety of car types complicates the selection of an "average" capacity. Box car capacity was used as the standard in lieu of a more complex index of various car types. Box cars contributed the largest percentage of all freight cars over the period: 39% in 1880; 41% in 1890; and 44% in 1914.[16] The average capacity in tons of all freight cars by type in 1914 was 35 for box cars, 36 for flat cars, 31 for stock cars, and 51 for coal cars.[17] Since coal cars contributed the second highest percentage of all freight cars (38% in 1914) the absolute capacity obtained from box cars alone understates the capacity for all cars.[18] Fortunately box car capacity is a fair proxy for freight cars other than coal, and coal represented a stable proportion of total cars over the period: 37% in 1880, 36% in 1890; and 38% in 1914.[19]

---

[16]10th U.S. Census, 1880; 11th U.S. Census, 1890; ICC, Statistics of Railways in the United States for 1914, p. 21.

[17]ICC, Ibid.

[18]Ibid.

[19]See note 16.

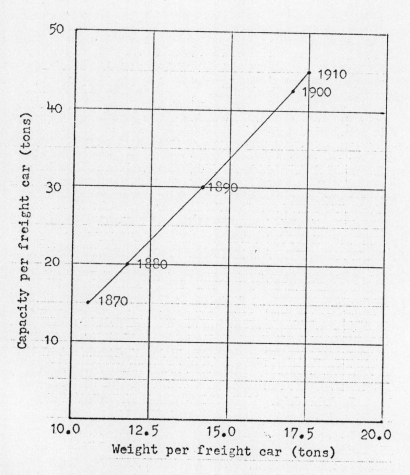

Fig. E2. - - Graph of freight car weight vs. capacity, 1870-1910

Therefore box car capacity should accurately trace the trend of capacity increases for all cars.

Figure E2 plots the capacity of new box cars versus car weight was compiled from a cross-section of the available data.[20] The semi-decadal estimates of car weights derived in Appendix D were used to obtain corresponding capacities for those years from the graph. The capacity index for freight cars is simply the ratio of the capacity in a given year to the capacity in 1910. As with locomotives increasing car weight brought increasing operating costs. Based on Wellington's data for locomotives and his observation of small increases in coal consumption with increases in car weight,[21] it was estimated that a doubling of freight car size would increase operating costs by ten percent. Using this estimate the operating costs for freight cars in any given year relative to operating costs in 1910 were computed based on relative weight changes. Dividing car capacity by this index of operating cost per car produced the index of freight car performance, as shown in column 7 of Table E2.

---

[20]A. M. Wellington, Location of the Railways, Op. Cit., pp. 114, 163, 485-6. Arthur T. Hadley, Railroad Transportation, Its History and Law, (New York: G. P. Putnam's Sons, 1899), p. 106. Kent T. Healy, "Development of a National System of Transportation," Growth of the American Economy (New York: Prentice Hall, 1944), pp. 521-551. Emery R. Johnson, Principles of Railroad Transportation (New York: Appleton and Co., 1920).

[21]A. M. Wellington, Location of the Railways, Op. Cit., p. 567.

Table E2

CAPITAL COMPONENT PERFORMANCE INDEXES 1910=100

Year	1	2	3	4	5	6	7	8	9
1870	45	5.2	85	41	15.0	92	36	46	70
1871	46			43			37		71
1872	47			44			38		71
1873	47			46			39		72
1874	48			47			40		73
1875	49	6.3	86	49	17.0	93	41		74
1876	50			51			42	49	74
1877	52			54			44		75
1878	53			56			45		76
1879	55			59			47		77
1880	56	8.0	88	61	20.0	93	48		78
1881	57			63			49		78
1882	59			65			50		79
1883	60			67			52		80
1884	62			69			53		81
1885	63	9.6	90	71	23.0	94	54		82
1886	65			73			57		82
1887	67			75			60		83
1888	68			77			63		84
1889	70			79			66		85
1890	72	11.2	92	81	30.0	96	69		86
1891	74			83			72	57	86
1892	76			84			75		87
1893	77			86			78		87
1894	79			87			81		87
1895	81	12.5	94	89	36.8	98	84		87
1896	84			89			86		88
1897	87			90			87		88
1898	89			90			89		88
1899	93			91			91		92
1900	95	13.5	98	91	42.5	99	93		97
1901	98			92			94		102
1902	100			93			95	70	106
1903	103			95			97		105
1904	105			96			98		103
1905	108	14.8	102	97	45.0	101	99		102
1906	106			97			99		100
1907	105			98			99	66	100
1908	103			99			100		100
1909	102			100			100		100
1910	100	15.0	100	100	45.0	100	100		100

256

Table E2 (Continued)

Year	1	2	3	4	5	6	7	8	9
1911	100			100			100		100
1912	100			100			100		100
1913	100			100			100		100
1914	100			100			100	66	100

Column   Description

1   Track index, 1910 = 100, derived as the ratio of the average weight of new locomotives in the current year to the weight in 1910. Weight estimates from Table D6 were linearly interpolated to obtain annual figures.

2   Average tractive power of new locomotives in tons derived from Figure E1 using weights from Table D6.

3   Locomotive operating cost index defined in the text.

4   Locomotive index, 1910 = 100, derived as the ratio of column 2 to the 1910 tractive power, 15.0, divided by the index of unit operating cost in column 3. Annual figures were obtained by linear interpolation

5   Freight car capacity in tons derived from Figure E1 using the semi-decadal weights in Table D6.

6   Freight car operating cost index, 1910 = 100, as defined in the text.

7   Freight car index, 1910 = 100, derived as car capacity in column 5 divided by 1910 capacity, 45.0 tons, all divided by the index of operating cost in column 6. Annual figures were obtained by linear interpolation.

8   Passenger car length in feet taken from sources discussed in the text. Four feet were subtracted from each length to adjust for vestibule area.

9   Passenger car index, 1910 = 100, derived by dividing the length in column 8 by the length in 1910.

Passenger Cars

The definition of the most significant measure of passenger car capacity is difficult. This is so because passenger "comfort" is an important factor but one which defies
precise measurement. After enumerating the more obvious
advances in toilet facilities, heating, suspension, and
lighting, one must simply observe that a measure of capacity
which abstracts from such factors understates the actual
increase in capacity.[22] On the positive side five quanti-
fiable measures of capacity may be suggested: car length;
car area; car volume; passenger capacity; and car weight.
Since car width and height varied very little over the period from 1870 to 1914, the first three measures are essentially the same.

As with freight cars the problem is further complicated
by the variety of cars classified as "passenger" cars. Ordinary coach cars accounted for roughly 70% of all passenger
cars through the period, while baggage cars contributed 25%
and sleeping, parlor, and dining cars made up the additional

---

[22]Edwin P. Alexander, The Pennsylvania Railroad (New
York: W. W. Norton and Co., 1947), pp. 93-95. Kincaid A.
Herb, The Louisville and Nashville Railroad (2nd rev ed,
Louisville: Louisville and Nashville Public Relations De-
partment, 1964), pp. 330-332. Rodney Hitt (ed), The Car
Builder's Dictionary (New York: The Railroad Gazette, 1906),
pp. 40-44. Hamilton Ellis, Nineteenth Century Railway
Carriages (London: Modern Transport Publishing Co., 1949).
Lucius Beebe, Mansions on Rails (Berkeley: Howell-North,
1959).

5%.[23]   Passenger capacity is a difficult concept to relate
to baggage cars, and while weight may be taken as a general
proxy for increased capacity it is more likely that increases
in car weight brought increasing returns to scale.   Therefore
the length of the passenger coach was used as a measure of
capacity for all passenger cars.[24]

A minor correction to floor length was required to account for the changing proportion of vestibule space over
time. An estimated length of four feet was subtracted from
the actual car length in each year, and the ratio of this
corrected length to the corrected length in 1910 was used as
the capacity index. No correction was made for increases
in operating cost per car with increases in weight in order
to compensate for the omission of corrections for passenger
comfort.

Summary

Table E2 traces the derivation of the performance indexes for track, locomotives, freight cars and passenger

---

[23]See note 16.

[24]Passenger car length was obtained from the following
sources:
    1870:   Kincaid A. Herb, The Louisville and Nashville
            Railroad, Op. Cit., p. 331.
    1876, 1891, 1898, 1902: Edwin A. Pratt, American Rail-
            ways, (London: MacMillan and Co., Ltd., 1903),
            p. 89.
    1906:   The Car Builder's Dictionary, Op. Cit., 1906,
            pp. 40-44.
    1914:   The Official Railway Equipment Register, Vol. 30,
            1914-15.

cars. The record of steady improvement in each component
is striking. Without any single dramatic technical leaps
efficiency more than doubled for locomotives, almost tripled
for freight cars and increased by more than fifty percent
for passenger cars. This impressive record was the result
of weight increases which brought sharp increases in capacity at small added operating costs. Those weight increases,
in turn, were made possible by a doubling of track strength
during the period produced by the replacement of iron rail
with steel and increases in rail weight. The major changes
in each index underscore the importance of including changing performance factors in an evaluation of capital capacity
and its impact on the investment decision.

APPENDIX F

AGGREGATE REGRESSION DATA, MODELS, AND RESULTS

Table F1

AGGREGATE REGRESSION DATA

Year	1	2	3	4	5	6	7	8	9	10	11	12	13	14	15	16
1872	545	51	495	1334	39	1295	174	64	191	127		618	760	87	35	104
1873	464	82	381	1490	84	1406	194	67	195	128		698	776	86	36	103
1874	258	25	233	1586	100	1436	215	67	198	131		680	753	79	35	94
1875	96	8	89	1627	106	1521	228	74	194	120		641	706	75	34	90
1876	126	12	114	1690	119	1570	241	68	195	127		702	668	73	32	85
1877	124	12	112	1763	134	1630	243	59	183	124		594	662	65	32	77
1878	150	19	131	1856	152	1704	256	54	196	142		515	645	63	29	74
1879	183	33	150	1971	184	1786	320	62	239	177		464	598	66	30	77
1880	314	40	274	2143	224	1919	330	77	292	215		464	560	72	32	65
1881	551	75	476	2455	295	2161	382	93	302	209		484	519	73	34	36
1882	556	65	491	2794	357	2437	412	51	305	203		507	524	73	35	86
1883	394	43	351	3063	403	2660	459	102	328	226		547	523	70	35	82
1884	249	19	231	3249	425	2824	390	94	285	191		613	515	67	35	78
1885	173	14	159	3383	443	2940	506	76	274	196		471	469	66	35	77
1886	237	31	206	3571	485	3087	541	82	307	225		375	455	69	37	81

Table F1 (Continued)

Year	1	2	3	4	5	6	7	8	9	10	11	12	13	14	15	16
1887	487	61	426	3955	563	3392	621	92	365	158		409	465	71	38	82
1888	418	44	375	4312	625	3687	658	80	311	231		384	459	69	40	78
1889	291	40	252	4583	690	3893	695	81	325	244		335	443	69	41	78
1890	162	10	152	4732	718	4015	782	86	342	256	106	354	455	71	43	81
1891	114	28	86	4855	768	4087	844	91	344	253	114	383	471	72	44	81
1892	101	17	84	4978	819	4159	903	98	353	260	120	377	453	72	46	82
1893	354	40	313	5364	923	4441	958	101	358	257	114	435	465	72	49	80
1894	328	103	224	5752	1091	4660	859	96	305	210	60	417	441	69	49	76
1895	80	-9	89	5840	1090	4751	869	85	311	226	60	350	427	70	51	76
1896	174	-7	168	6031	1110	4921	961	88	339	251	95	377	434	72	52	79
1897	42	-20	63	6083	1089	4994	941	87	328	241	86	347	411	68	56	73
1898	82	12	70	6204	1126	5078	1104	96	387	291	147	338	403	70	59	73
1899	146	17	130	6400	1179	5222	1199	111	412	301	177	303	385	73	65	70
1900	287	41	245	6743	1260	5483	1355	140	481	341	253	393	389	78	64	83
1901	264	99	165	7097	1426	5671	1417	156	511	354	273	325	383	82	75	85
1902	318	82	236	7505	1564	5941	1536	185	560	375	315	321	384	85	81	86
1903	386	118	269	7969	1721	6247	1679	197	590	393	338	390	403	86	82	88
1904	446	79	367	8489	1815	6673	1708	222	579	357	317	385	398	90	87	91
1905	326	61	266	8877	1890	6987	1837	238	633	395	365	320	389	95	93	93
1906	444	144	300	9376	2055	7321	2082	273	720	447	434	358	400	97	99	97
1907	514	193	322	9948	2289	7658	2283	308	777	469	488	521	427	101	101	101
1908	308	136	172	10292	2453	7839	2157	391	635	244	444	497	422	100	104	99
1909	260	-2	262	10596	2478	8118	2157	321	710	389	441	447	407	98	105	96
1910	385	87	298	10995	2579	8416	2482	406	805	399	583	463	418	100	100	100
1911	443	108	335	11453	2706	8747	2487	460	745	285	547	468	419	102	104	101

Table F1 (Continued)

Year	1	2	3	4	5	6	7	8	9	10	11	12	13	14	15	16
1912	293	48	245	11758	2769	8989	2564	400	727	327	453	473	423	104	110	101
1913	349	95	254	12118	2890	9228	2854	369	805	436	547	516	444	103	109	106
1914	306	78	228	12454	3009	9445	2795	362	674	223	395	464	444	105	103	106

Variable Description

Column

1   Gross investment in track and equipment in millions of current dollars.[a] Details may not add to totals due to rounding.

2   Gross investment in equipment in millions of current dollars.[a]

3   Gross investment in track in millions of current dollars.[a]

4   Gross track and equipment capital stock in millions of 1910 dollars.[a]

5   Gross equipment capital stock in millions of 1910 dollars.[a]

6   Gross track capital stock in millions of 1910 dollars.[a]

7   Gross output in millions of 1910 dollars from Table A3.

8   Capacity pressure, defined as the minimum prior ratio of gross capital to gross output multiplied by current output, in millions of 1910 dollars.

9   Net operating revenue in millions of current dollars from column 5 of Table A1.

Table F1 (Continued)

Column	Variable Description
10	Retained earnings in millions of current dollars, defined as net operating revenue from column 9 minus annual dividends from Poor's Manual of the Railroads for 1871 to 1890, and from the Bureau of the Census, Historical Statistics, Series Q41 and Q115, pp. 428, 434, for 1890 to 1914.
11	Net revenue in millions of current dollars from Historical Statistics, Series Q113, p. 434.
12	Equity yield per cent from Historical Statistics, Series X337, p. 656.
13	Bond rate per cent from Historical Statistics, Series X332, p. 656.
14	Capital price index, 1910 = 100.[b]
15	Equipment price index, 1910 = 100.[b]
16	Track price index, 1910 = 100.[b]

[a]Capital and investment series are derived in Appendix D.

[b]Price indexes are derived in Appendix C.

Table F2

VARIABLE NOTATION

Symbol	Description
I	Gross investment in current dollars.
K	Gross capital stock in constant dollars.
X	Link relative gross output index times 1910 output.
DX	Annual Change in gross output in constant dollars.
CAP	Capacity pressure defined as the minimum previous ratio of gross capital to output multiplied by current output.

Table F2 (Continued)

Symbol	Description
TM	Ton-mileage of freight carried.
DTM	Annual change in ton-mileage of freight carried.
GROSS E	Gross Earnings in current dollars.
NOR	Net operating revenue in current dollars.
RET E	Retained earnings in current dollars.
NR	Net revenue in current dollars.
AGE	Number of years since initial firm charter.
EQ YLD	Equity yield.
BOND R	Bond rate.
P	Capital goods price index, 1910 = 100.
INTEREST	Annual fixed interest payments in current dollars.
Prefix A	Two year average of following variable.
-t	Variable lagged "t" years.

Table F3

AGGREGATE MODEL ESTIMATES

Model[a]	a_1[b]	a_2	a_3	a_4	R^2[c]	DW[d]
1-1a	-.0023(5.1)	+.0961(.8)	-.2732(2.4)	+.0233(3.4)	.59	1.0
1-1b	-.0003(1.4)	+.0799(2.7)	-.3930(4.1)	+.0069(1.8)	.87	2.6
1-1c	-.0061(4.1)	+.0578(.5)	-.1863(2.2)	+.0132(3.1)	.59	.9
1-1d	+.0001(.2)	+.0069(.2)	-.3384(3.2)	+.0049(1.1)	.67	2.2
1-1e	-.0069(2.1)	+.0149(.7)	-.0731(1.3)	+.0231(2.2)	.34	1.2
1-1f	-.0012(2.3)	+.0645(4.5)	-.1109(1.6)	+.0044(3.0)	.81	2.1
1-2a	-.0727(3.5)	-3.3562(.7)	+.0313(2.6)		.42	1.1
1-2b	+.0210(4.1)	-13.8267(3.8)	+.0072(2.8)		.80	1.4
1-2c	-.0668(3.8)	-3.0215(.8)	+.0283(2.8)		.47	1.1
1-2d	+.0169(3.4)	-9.8462(2.9)	+.0016(.6)		.62	1.3
1-2e	-.0059(1.3)	-.3321(.3)	+.0031(1.1)		.13	1.7
1-2f	+.0044(2.1)	-3.9678(2.7)	+.0057(5.3)		.83	2.1
1-3a	+.5967(3.5)	-.0126(.7)	+.0548(.9)	+.1032(1.8)	.46	1.4
1-3b	+.7062(4.1)	+.0002(.1)	+.0606(4.1)	+.0373(2.4)	.78	2.1
1-3c	+.3015(2.9)	+.1214(1.5)	+.0608(1.1)	+.1264(2.2)	.38	1.6
1-3d	+.8846(2.5)	+.0314(1.1)	+.0447(2.9)	+.0155(1.1)	.59	1.5
1-3e	+.2297(.9)	-.0058(.3)	-.0089(.7)	+.0241(1.8)	.21	2.1
1-3f	+.7323(5.8)	-.0082(.8)	+.0363(6.8)	+.0308(5.8)	.88	2.8
1-4a	-.0032(2.5)	+.3232(2.6)	+.0133(.1)	-36.3341(2.2)	.32	1.2
1-4b	-.0002(.7)	+.0703(1.2)	+.0228(.6)	-5.3848(1.4)	.40	1.6
1-4c	-.0066(2.4)	+.1376(2.6)	-.0187(.2)	-.6324(1.0)	.28	1.2
1-4d	-.0017(1.6)	+.0868(2.0)	+.0352(1.4)	-6.6495(2.2)	.47	1.8

Table F3 (Continued)

Model	a_1	a_2	a_3	a_4	R^2	DW
1-4e	+.0005(.3)	+.0267(1.7)	+.0176(1.0)	+.1196(1.1)	.19	1.7
1-4f	+.0001(.1)	-.0173(.5)	-.0169(.9)	+.1131(.1)	.36	1.4
1-5a	-.0004(1.2)	+.0534(1.6)			.13	1.6
1-5b	+.0002(1.6)	-.0132(1.2)			.30	1.1
1-5c	-.0051(2.3)	+.1287(2.5)			.24	1.0
1-5d	+.0005(1.6)	-.0089(1.3)			.22	1.4
1-5e	+.0001(.2)	+.0173(1.3)			.11	1.3
1-5f	+.0001(.4)	-.0131(2.4)			.33	1.4
1-6a	+.0002(.4)	-.1003(1.0)			.05	1.0
1-6b	-.0006(2.7)	+.1427(3.8)			.55	1.9
1-6c	+.0010(.6)	-.1067(1.3)			.08	1.0
1-6d	-.0013(2.1)	+.0872(3.0)			.45	2.1
1-6e	-.0006(.9)	+.0081(.3)			.04	1.3
1-6f	-.0007(1.8)	+.0558(2.6)			.35	1.8

aThe numbers designate the basic model and the letter refers to the capital component used as the dependent variable and the period of the regression. The symbols used in the following equations are explained in the text and in Table F2.

Structure

Model	
1-1	$I/P = a_0 + a_1 K_{-1} + a_2 NOR/P_{-1} + a_3 BOND\ R_{-1} + a_4 P_{-1}$
1-2	$I = a_0 + a_1 X_{-1} + a_2 EQ\ YLD_{-1} + a_3 RET\ E_{-1}$
1-3	$I = a_0 + a_1 I_{-1} + a_2 K_{-1} + a_3 DX + a_4 DX_{-1}$

Table F3 (Continued)

Model	Structure

1-4 $\quad I/P = a_0 + a_1 K_{-2} + a_2 NOR/P_{-2} + a_3 DNOR/P_{-1} + a_4 NOR/K_{-2}$

1-5 $\quad I/P = a_0 + a_1 K_{-1} + a_2 NOR/P_{-2}$

1-6 $\quad I/P = a_0 + a_1 K_{-1} + a_2 NR/P_{-1}$

Subscript	Component	Period
a	Total	1872-1895
b	Total	1896-1914
c	Track	1872-1895
d	Track	1896-1914
e	Equipment	1872-1895
f	Equipment	1896-1914

[b]Columns a_1 - a_4 list the ordinary least squares coefficient estimate followed by the "t" statistic for that coefficient in parentheses.

[c]The R^2 listed is the squared coefficient of multiple correlation corrected for the number of degrees of freedom.

[d]The Durbin-Watson coefficient.

APPENDIX G

SAMPLE RAILROAD COMPANIES

Introduction

The selection of a representative sample of companies
from the railroad sector for a period approaching half a
century is a complex task. The changing corporate structure and the increasing pattern of consolidation and inter-
locking control over the period makes even the formulation
of a consistent definition of individual firms difficult.
Moreover the sample was selected to trace the changing
composition of the industry in terms of regional and size
distribution. The selection process was founded on a
series of compromises. Companies were defined to be single
corporate structures which exercised direct control over the
operational and investment policies of a railroad network.
Companies whose equity was controlled by another firm retained their individual status unless operational control
was transferred. On the other hand sections of road leased
for long periods of time were considered as integral parts
of the leasee. These definitional distinctions become
weaker after the consolidation movement of the late 1890s,
since the degree of operational control exercised by parent
systems is difficult to measure. Part of the selection

process for the sample was to minimize such exceptions to
the clear application of the firm definition. Most sample
roads developed some system affiliation, but each road continued to exercise individual operational control.

Sample Selection

The sample of 19 companies reflects the shifting composition of road mileage in the sector due to regional expansion. A spectrum of firm sizes are also included
extending from the Central of Georgia and the Maine Central
through the larger trunk lines and transcontinental systems.
The sample is somewhat biased in that each firm survived
in some form throughout the period from 1870 to 1914. Several of them underwent vast reorganizations, however, and
in this sense they reflect the cyclical instability of the
sector. The sample size was limited to 19 by the difficulties of company integrity, firm survival over the period
and data collection. The companies selected are listed in
Table G1 with their identification numbers used in the
statistical analysis.

Annual observations on 25 variables were recorded for
each company over the 45 year period from 1870 to 1914.[1]

---

[1]Data were collected from the annual reports recorded by
Henry Poor, Manual of the Railroads, for 1873 to 1915.
Poor's data were compared with available company annual reports where inconsistencies or omissions were discovered in
his annual data.

Table G1

SAMPLE COMPANY CLASSIFICATION

Number	Name	Charter	Region[a]	System[b]	Receivership
1	Boston and Maine	1835	1	1	
2	Maine Central	1862	1	1	
3	New York, New Haven and Hartford	1872	1	1	
4	Baltimore and Ohio	1827	2	1	1896-8
5	New York Central	1869	2	3	
6	New York, Lake Erie and Western	1861	2	1	1875-8,1883-5
7	Pennsylvania	1848	2	0	
8	Central of Georgia	1867	3	1,2[c]	1892-6
9	Chicago and Northwestern	1859	4	3	
10	Chicago, Burlington and Quincy	1851	4	4	
11	Chicago, Milwaukee and St. Paul	1863	4	1	
12	Illinois Central	1851	3	2	
13	Michigan Central	1846	2	3	
14	Louisville and Nashville	1850	3	0	
15	Mobile and Ohio	1848	3	0	1875-82
16	Union Pacific	1862	5	0	1893-7
17	Atchison, Topeka and Santa Fe	1863	5	2	1893-5
18	Northern Pacific	1864	4	1	1874-5,1884,1893-6
19	Missouri Pacific	1849	5	0	1876-8,1888,1911

[a]Regional classifications are depicted in Figure G1.

[b]System 1 refers to roads controlled by the Morgan group, 2 to Harriman, 3 to Vanderbilt, 4 to Hill, and 0 to no system affiliation.

[c]Controlled by Morgan from 1895 to 1909 and by Harriman from 1909 to 1914.

In addition to earnings, output, and physical capital component series, several financial variables including dividends, cash on hand, funded debt, interest payments, equity
issued and surplus were collected. Several variables were
also recorded for use as dummy variables in regression
analysis including the region in which the company operated,
the system to which it belonged, and whether it was operated by a receiver, underwent a merger, or was reorganized
in a given year. If the firm reported data in December
all annual figures were averaged to produce June estimates.

The distribution of companies into regions was based
on combinations of ICC regions for 1900[2] with minor adjustments to reduce the number of regions from ten to five.
Figure G1 outlines the five regions used in the analysis
and Table G1 classifies each company by region. Where
companies extended into more than one region the classification was based on the region containing the largest percentage of total company track mileage. Table G1 also
classifies each company by its parent system in the period
from 1895 to 1914. Four system divisions were made based
on E. G. Campbell's analysis of controlling interests:

---

[2]ICC, Statistics of Railways in the United States, 1900,
Op. Cit., p. i.

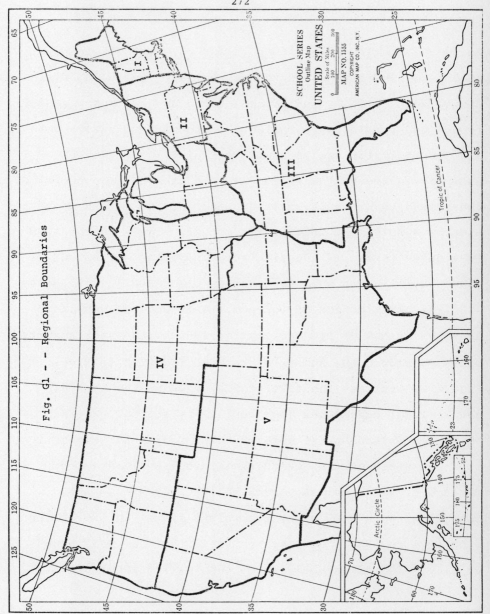

Fig. G1 - - Regional Boundaries

SCHOOL SERIES
Outline Map
UNITED STATES
Scale of Miles
MAP NO. 1555
COPYRIGHT
AMERICAN MAP CO., INC., N.Y.

(1) Morgan, (2) Harriman, (3) Vanderbilt, (4) Hill.[3] These
systems controlled a large proportion of all roads in this
period and 16 of the 19 sample firms fell under their control. The neat system classifications do not reflect the
overlapping control and shifting detentes among systems,
but the distinctions in operational control are substantially
valid. System and regional dummy variables were introduced
in cross-section equations to adjust for the variation in
investment behavior resulting from company location or
system affiliation.

Sample Characteristics

At best the final selection of companies is the product
of numerous compromises of the attempts to select firms with
continuous corporate structure, complete recorded data, and
representative regional and size distribution. Despite
those difficulties the companies are generally typical of
the sector as a whole in the period from 1870 to 1914.
Attempts to estimate output and equipment totals for the
entire industry by scaling sample totals in the period from
1870 to 1890, as discussed in Appendixes A and D respectively,
indicated that the sample did reflect aggregate trends accurately. The total gross earnings of the sample represented

---

[3]E. G. Campbell, The Reorganization of the American
Railroad System, 1893-1900 (New York: Columbia University
Press, 1938).

30.2% of the gross earnings of the sector in 1870, 34.4% in 1880, 32.8% in 1890, 42.7% in 1900, and 41.5% in 1910. Those percentages are higher than the corresponding proportion of total railroad capital controlled by the sample companies as shown in Table D6. The increase in proportionate representation in the later years and the high earnings levels are indicative of the bias in the sample since each firm survived the period of extensive consolidation at the end of the nineteenth century.

The regional distribution of roads closely parallels the regional expansion of the sector. Five of the companies were located in region 2, including the four major east-west trunk lines from the Middle Atlantic to Chicago. The three lines in region 1, New England, were principally local carriers with the exception of the New York, New Haven, and Hartford which underwent rapid expansion after 1895 under Morgan's direction. The four southern roads of region 3 included the large network of the Illinois Central and the strong Louisville and Nashville as well as two weaker roads, the Mobile and Ohio and the Georgia Central. Three of the four roads in region 4 centered on the agricultural trade with Chicago and were apparently well managed. The fourth, the Northern Pacific, had a more sordid history and played a major role in the crises of 1873, 1884, and 1893. The major transcontinental systems in the sample,

excluding the Northern Pacific, were located in region 5.
All three roads in that region experienced rapid growth
through the period, but that growth was often marred by
financial failures.

Most of the roads, 11 of the 19, endured the period
from 1870 to 1914 without being forced into receivership.
Four lines, the Erie, the Mobile and Ohio, the Northern
Pacific, and the Missouri Pacific, were reorganized in the
depression following the crisis of 1873, but only one, the
Northern Pacific, went under in the crisis of 1884. Six
of the sample roads entered receivership in the depression
of the 1890s. The Northern Pacific went in the first wave
of failures in 1893, largely due to its heavy capitalization
and high fixed interest payments. The Atchison, the Union
Pacific, and the Erie also entered receivership in 1893.
The Atchison went under because of excessive bond issues
in the face of competition by Gould's Missouri Pacific, the
Union Pacific due to its approaching government loan repayment and poor earnings on a number of branches, and the Erie
because of its financial restrictions which forced the creation of a large and cumbersome floating debt. The Georgia
Central went into receivership after a series of complex
litigations following its acquisition by the Richmond and
West Point Terminal Company. Finally, in 1896 the venerable
Baltimore and Ohio, hurt by the payment of unearned dividends

and the failure of earlier attempts at reorganization, also entered receivership.[4] This wave of receiverships and subsequent reorganizations contributed to the realignment of the sector into a number of large systems. Four of the six roads which entered receivership in the 1890s were reorganized by Morgan, and two, the Union Pacific and the Atchison, by Harriman.

The impact of control by different systems on the sample was largely regional. Morgan's control centered on the roads in regions 1 and 3, although it extended to the Chicago, Milwaukee and St. Paul, and the Northern Pacific as well. Eight of the sample roads fell under his control in the period from 1895 to 1914, while four were controlled by Harriman at some point, three by Vanderbilt, and one by Hill. Harriman's base was the Illinois Central and the remainder of the system was largely directed at control of transcontinental outlets, while Vanderbilt's primary road was the New York Central and the remainder of the system operated largely as feeder lines to that road. Hill's influence on the sample extended beyond the Burlington, and after 1901 a community of interest in the control of roads north of Chicago existed among Harriman, Hill, and Morgan. A similar detente existed in the East between Morgan and Vanderbilt and often included the Pennsylvania system as well.

---

[4]Ibid, pp. 30-62, 83, 92, 128.

Summary

The sample thus reflects the major trends which impacted on the sector as a whole. The regional distribution follows the pattern of national expansion due to the inclusion of several rapidly expanding western roads. Most of the principal systems which emerged after 1895 are represented so that the impact of reorganization and system control on investment can be examined. The sample represents a large and increasing part of the entire sector, contributing roughly 21 percent of gross capital and 30 percent of gross earnings in 1870 and 37 percent of capital and 42 percent of earnings in 1910. While the sample is limited to 19 companies, it should accurately reflect the investment behavior of the sector as a whole.

APPENDIX H

COMPANY INVESTMENT MODELS AND REGRESSION RESULTS

Table H1

SUMMARY OF COMPANY CROSS SECTION MODEL ESTIMATES

Model[a]	a_1[b]	a_2	a_3	a_4	R^{2c}
3-3-1a	+.0438(8,8,10)	+.0007(1,3,4)	+.0301(5,6,8)		.51
3-3-1b	+.0540(3,3,4)	+.0009(1,3,4)	+.0895(3,3,4)		.52
3-3-1c	+.0411(5,5,6)	+.0002(0,0,0)	+.0219(2,3,4)		.51
3-3-1d	+.0427(5,5,5)	+.0008(0,1,2)	+.0169(3,3,4)		.47
3-3-1e	+.0454(3,3,5)	+.0007(1,2,2)	+.0596(2,3,4)		.56
3-3-2a	+.0411(7,9,9)	+.0001(2,3,4)	+.0176(6,7,8)		.51
3-3-2b	+.0451(5,6,6)	+.0001(1,2,3)	+.0219(4,4,5)		.56
3-3-2c	+.0367(2,3,3)	+.0001(1,1,1)	+.0075(2,3,3)		.45
3-3-2d	+.0303(2,3,3)	−.0001(0,1,1)	+.0097(3,4,5)		.42
3-3-2e	+.0509(5,6,6)	+.0002(2,2,3)	+.0212(3,3,3)		.59
3-3-3a	+.0298(5,8,10)	+.0010(3,4,5)	+.0077(5,6,6)		.47
3-3-3b	+.0512(2,4,4)	+.0012(2,3,4)	+.0735(3,3,3)		.48
3-3-3c	+.0267(3,4,6)	+.0007(1,1,1)	+.0048(2,3,3)		.46
3-3-3d	+.0316(3,4,5)	+.0007(1,1,1)	+.0044(3,3,3)		.42
3-3-3e	+.0279(2,4,5)	+.0012(2,3,4)	+.0134(2,3,3)		.52

Table H1 (Continued)

Model	a_1	a_2	a_3	a_4	R^2
3-6-1a	+.0545(5,6,8)	+.0189(1,2,3)	+.0032(1,1,1)	-.0003(3,3,5)	.49
3-6-1b	+.0675(2,3,4)	+.0237(0,1,2)	+.0032(0,0,0)	-.0005(2,2,2)	.46
3-6-1c	+.0596(3,3,4)	+.0147(1,1,1)	+.0093(1,1,1)	-.0001(1,1,3)	.53
3-6-1d	+.0493(3,3,4)	+.0203(1,1,1)	+.0030(0,0,0)	-.0004(2,2,3)	.48
3-6-1e	+.0677(2,3,4)	+.0166(0,1,2)	+.0356(1,1,1)	-.0001(1,1,2)	.50
3-6-2a	+.0740(6,7,8)	+.0018(1,4,4)	+.0001(0,2,2)	-.0001(4,4,5)	.51
3-6-2b	+.0862(4,5,6)	+.0017(0,2,2)	+.0001(0,1,1)	-.0001(2,2,3)	.55
3-6-2c	+.0616(2,2,2)	+.0021(1,2,2)	+.0051(0,1,1)	-.0001(2,2,2)	.47
3-6-2d	+.0503(2,2,2)	-.0005(0,0,0)	+.0001(0,1,1)	-.0001(2,2,2)	.43
3-6-2e	+.0905(4,5,6)	+.0029(1,3,3)	-.0054(1,1,2)	-.0001(1,1,2)	.60
3-6-3a	+.0255(4,4,5)	+.0166(1,2,3)	+.0029(1,1,1)	-.0002(3,3,4)	.48
3-6-3b	+.0577(2,2,3)	+.0200(0,1,1)	+.0032(0,0,0)	-.0004(2,2,2)	.49
3-6-3c	+.0197(2,2,2)	+.0154(1,1,2)	-.0414(1,1,1)	-.0001(1,1,2)	.48
3-6-3d	+.0319(2,2,2)	+.0146(0,0,1)	+.0032(0,0,0)	-.0002(2,2,2)	.49
3-6-3e	+.0218(2,2,3)	+.0180(1,2,2)	-.0351(1,2,2)	-.0002(1,1,2)	.48
3-7-1a	+.0294(3,4,7)	+.0150(2,4,5)	+.0025(1,1,3)	-.0003(2,4,5)	.50
3-7-1b	+.0755(2,3,4)	+.0137(0,2,3)	+.0025(0,0,2)	-.0007(1,2,2)	.46
3-7-1c	+.0136(1,1,3)	+.0155(2,2,2)	-.0063(1,1,2)	-.0001(1,2,2)	.56
3-7-1d	+.0408(2,2,3)	+.0119(1,3,4)	+.0042(0,0,2)	-.0003(2,2,2)	.49
3-7-1e	+.0212(1,2,4)	+.0176(1,1,1)	-.0197(2,3,3)	-.0003(0,2,3)	.52
3-7-2a	+.0500(5,5,6)	+.0026(2,3,4)	+.0003(1,1,1)	-.0001(3,5,7)	.52
3-7-2b	+.0555(4,4,5)	+.0022(0,1,2)	+.0003(1,1,1)	-.0001(1,3,5)	.55
3-7-2c	+.0330(1,1,1)	+.0046(2,2,2)	-.0169(1,1,2)	-.0001(2,2,2)	.48
3-7-2d	+.0258(1,1,2)	+.0031(1,1,2)	+.0003(1,1,1)	-.0001(1,1,2)	.45
3-7-2e	+.0633(4,4,4)	+.0024(1,2,2)	-.0041(0,1,3)	-.0001(2,4,5)	.59

Table H1 (Continued)

Model	a_1	a_2	a_3	a_4	R^2
3-7-3a	+.0194(3,3,5)	+.0069(3,4,6)	+.0040(1,2,2)	-.0003(3,4,4)	.47
3-7-3b	+.0712(2,2,3)	+.0127(0,1,3)	+.0042(0,1,1)	-.0006(2,2,2)	.44
3-7-3c	+.0120(1,1,2)	+.0063(3,3,3)	-.0261(1,1,1)	-.0001(1,2,2)	.50
3-7-3d	+.0269(2,2,2)	+.0065(1,2,4)	+.0042(0,1,1)	-.0004(1,2,2)	.45
3-7-3e	+.0146(1,1,3)	+.0072(2,2,2)	-.0215(1,2,2)	-.0003(2,2,2)	.48

[a]The numbers listed designate the basic model followed by the capital component used as the dependent variable, while the letter indicates the period for which cross sections were grouped for the summary equation shown. In addition to the model structures shown below all models also included dummy variables for each company which indicated the company's region and parent system. The symbols used for the variables in the following equations are explained in the text and in Table F2.

Model	Structure
3-3	$AI = a_0 + a_1K_{-1} + a_2CAP_{-1} + a_3DTM_{-1}$
3-6	$AI = a_0 + a_1K_{-1} + a_2NOR_{-1} + a_3AGE + a_4INTEREST_{-1}$
3-7	$AI = a_0 + a_1K_{-1} + a_2GROSS\ E_{-1} + a_3AGE + a_4INTEREST_{-1}$

Subscript-Component		Number of Regressions
1	Total	
2	Equipment	9
3	Track	9

Subscript-Period		Number of Regressions
a	1871-1914	18
b	1871-1895	10
c	1895-1914	8

Subscript-Period	
d	Recession
e	Expansion

Table H1 (Continued)

^{b}The coefficients a_1-a_4 represent a weighted sum of the individual cross section results, where the weights are proportional to the reciprocal of the coefficient variance. The weighted coefficient is followed by the number of cross sections in which the coefficient was significant at the 98, 95, and 90 per cent confidence levels enclosed in parentheses.

^{c}The R^2 listed is the mean of the squared coefficients of multiple correlation of the individual cross sections corrected for the number of degrees of freedom.

Table H2

SUMMARY OF COMPANY TIME SERIES MODEL ESTIMATES

Model[a]	a_1[b]	a_2	a_3	a_4	R^2[c]
2-1-1a	-.0144(2,3,3)	+.0236(2,3,3)	+.0135(2,2,5)	+.0135(2,2,5)	.38
2-1-1b	+.0136(4,4,6)	-.0108(2,4,5)	-.4292(5,5,6)	+.0648(6,7,10)	.60
2-1-2a	+.0138(2,3,3)	-.0004(3,3,3)	-.0529(2,2,3)	+.0182(4,4,5)	.54
2-1-2b	-.0354(4,5,6)	+.0035(3,5,6)	-.1891(4,4,5)	+.0169(6,7,9)	.61
2-1-3a	-.0317(2,3,3)	+.0288(2,3,5)	+.2439(0,1,1)	+.1384(2,3,4)	.35
2-1-3b	-.0119(3,4,5)	+.0045(3,3,4)	-1.4179(5,7,8)	+.0400(6,6,7)	.78
2-2-1a	-.0011(4,5,5)	-.0227(6,7,9)	-.6056(6,8,9)	+.0987(9,11,13)	.45
2-2-1b	-.0002(7,7,8)	+.0048(3,5,6)	-.5268(3,5,6)	+.0420(5,6,8)	.63
2-2-2a	-.0035(5,6,7)	-.1536(9,11,13)	-.0001(0,2,4)	+.0371(13,14,14)	.60
2-2-2b	+.0055(7,8,8)	-.2503(5,5,6)	-.0001(3,5,5)	+.0106(5,5,6)	.61
2-2-3a	-.0192(3,5,6)	-.5934(5,6,7)	-.0010(5,5,5)	+.0592(7,10,12)	.40
2-2-3b	+.0031(5,5,5)	-.3919(4,5,5)	-.0002(7,9,9)	+.0343(6,7,10)	.56

Table H2 (Continued)

Model	a_1	a_2	a_3	a_4	R^2
2-3-1a	+.0189(2,4,4)	+.0020(4,4,6)	+.1409(8,10,11)		.42
2-3-1b	+.0387(6,12,12)	-.0004(2,3,5)	+.0091(2,2,3)		.54
2-3-2a	+.0478(8,10,11)	+.0002(1,1,2)	+.0183(9,10,13)		.57
2-3-2b	+.0461(9,10,10)	-.0001(2,4,5)	+.0123(4,5,5)		.59
2-3-3a	-.0013(0,1,2)	+.0020(4,4,7)	+.1140(7,8,9)		.33
2-3-3b	+.0295(6,6,9)	-.0001(2,2,3)	-.0032(1,2,3)		.43
2-4-1a	+.0307(2,2,4)	+.0036(1,2,4)	+.1150(11,11,13)		.46
2-4-1b	+.0227(4,5,6)	+.0018(6,6,6)	+.4206(12,13,15)		.67
2-4-2a	+.0010(3,3,4)	+.0043(4,4,6)	+.3871(10,11,12)		.62
2-4-2b	-.0729(4,6,9)	+.0001(7,8,12)	+.4904(13,16,17)		.64
2-4-3a	+.0358(2,2,2)	-.0007(2,2,2)	+.0964(10,10,11)		.41
2-4-3b	+.0124(4,4,6)	+.0012(4,4,5)	+.4406(10,10,13)		.61
2-1-4a	-.003?(4,4,5)	+.0007(5,5,5)	+.0962(2,3,4)	+.0206(5,5,6)	.55
2-1-4b	+.0158(3,4,4)	-.0184(9,10,12)	+.4098(5,6,7)	+.0112(8,10,11)	.66
2-1-5a	+.0187(3,3,4)	+.0057(5,5,6)	-.0236(2,4,6)	+.0029(3,4,7)	.61
2-1-5b	-.0054(4,5,6)	+.0014(3,4,4)	-.2213(7,7,7)	+.0172(9,9,9)	.80
2-3-4a	+.0146(4,5,6)	+.0012(8,9,9)	+.0018(3,4,5)		.48
2-3-4b	+.0283(9,13,13)	+.0003(2,2,2)	+.0116(4,5,7)		.50
2-3-5a	+.0454(8,8,9)	+.0004(4,6,7)	+.0079(4,6,9)		.56
2-3-5b	+.0378(7,7,7)	-.0001(4,5,5)	+.0031(3,3,4)		.70
2-4-4a	+.0585(7,8,8)	-.0046(3,4,5)	+.0226(7,9,10)		.47
2-4-4b	+.0209(6,6,6)	+.0018(2,6,6)	+.0778(8,10,10)		.56
2-4-5a	+.0371(3,3,3)	+.0003(8,9,9)	+.0504(18,18,18)		.70
2-4-5b	-.0079(5,6,7)	+.0024(7,8,9)	+.4642(18,18,18)		.83

Table H2 (Continued)

Model	a_1	a_2	a_3	R^2
2-5-4a	+.0058(5,5,5)	+.0920(8,8,8)	-.0009(7,8,9)	.47
2-5-4b	+.0236(6,7,8)	+.3327(3,5,7)	-.0001(5,6,7)	.50
2-5-5a	+.0491(9,9,9)	-.0009(3,3,3)	-.0001(6,7,7)	.55
2-5-5b	+.0291(11,11,12)	+.0222(4,5,6)	-.0001(4,4,4)	.69

[a]The numbers listed designate the basic model followed by the capital component used as the dependent variable, while the letter indicates the period for which the nineteen individual company time series results were grouped for the summary equation shown. In addition to the model structures shown below all models included dummy variables to account for changes in system affiliation. The symbols used for the variables in the following equations are explained in the text and in Table F2. For main track and other track the dependent variable was a three year average of investment and the independent variables were two year averages.

Model	Structure		Subscript-Component	
2-1	$AI = a_0 + a_1 K_{-1} + a_2 NOR_{-1} + a_3 BOND\ R_{-1} + a_4 P_{-1}$		1	Total
2-2	$AI = a_0 + a_1 TM_{-1} + a_2 EQ\ YLD_{-1} + a_3 RET\ E_{-1} + a_4 P_{-1}$		2	Equipment
2-3	$AI = a_0 + a_1 K_{-1} + a_2 CAP_{-1} + a_3 DTM_{-1}$		3	All Track
2-4	$AI = a_0 + a_1 K_{-1} + a_2 TM_{-1} + a_3 AI_{-1}$		4	Main Track
2-5	$AI = a_0 + a_1 K_{-1} + a_2 EQ\ YLD_{-1} + a_3 RET\ E_{-1}$		5	Other Track

Table H2 (Continued)

Subscript – Period

a   1871–1895
b   1896–1914

[b]The coefficients a_1–a_4 represent a weighted sum of the individual time series results, where the weights are proportional to the reciprocal of the coefficient variance. The weighted coefficient is followed by the number of company time series in which the coefficient was significant at the 98, 95, and 90 per cent confidence levels enclosed in parentheses.

[c]The R^2 listed is the mean of the squared coefficients of multiple correlation of the individual time series corrected for the number of degrees of freedom.

Table H3

REGIONAL SUMMARY OF TIME SERIES MODEL ESTIMATES

Model[a]	Region[b]	a_1		a_2		a_3		a_4		R^{2}[c]
2-1-3a	1	-.03	(1,1,1)	+.06	(2,2,3)	+ .43	(0,1,1)	-.02	(0,0,0)	.46
	2	+.06	(1,1,1)	-.14	(2,2,3)	- .12	(0,0,0)	+.13	(1,2,2)	.32
	3	+.003	(0,0,0)	-.05	(0,0,0)	- .03	(0,0,0)	+.05	(0,0,0)	.23
	4-5	-.07	(1,2,2)	+.06	(0,1,2)	-2.24	(1,1,1)	+.24	(1,1,2)	.40
2-1-3b	1	+.11	(1,1,1)	+.07	(1,1,1)	-1.51	(2,3,3)	+.06	(1,1,1)	.95
	2	-.03	(2,2,2)	+.03	(1,1,2)	-2.05	(3,3,3)	+.01	(2,2,2)	.65

Table H3 (Continued)

Model	Region	a_1	a_2	a_3	a_4	R^2
2-1-3b	3	-.03 (0,1,2)	+.01 (1,1,1)	-.30 (0,2,2)	+.03 (1,1,2)	.54
	4	+.02 (0,1,1)	-.05 (1,2,2)	-2.75 (1,1,1)	+.23 (1,1,1)	.46
	5	+.002 (1,1,1)	+.009 (1,1,1)	+1.90 (1,1,1)	+.04 (1,1,1)	.55
2-3-3a	1	+.005 (0,0,0)	+.002 (0,0,0)	+.14 (1,1,1)		.45
	2	+.03 (1,2,2)	+.0002 (0,0,1)	+.11 (4,4,4)		.36
	3	+.01 (0,0,0)	+.005 (0,0,0)	+.03 (0,0,0)		.28
	4-5	-.01 (0,0,1)	+.006 (0,0,0)	+.17 (0,0,0)		.27
2-3-3b	1	+.07 (0,0,1)	-.002 (0,0,0)	+.02 (1,1,1)		.27
	2	+.02 (1,1,1)	+.006 (1,1,1)	-.005 (0,1,1)		.55
	3	+.02 (1,1,1)	+.006 (1,1,1)	-.016 (1,1,1)		.49
	4	+.03 (2,2,2)	-.001 (1,1,1)	+.003 (0,0,0)		.37
	5	+.04 (2,2,3)	-.0006 (0,0,1)	-.001 (0,0,0)		.38
2-1-2a	1	+.06 (1,2,2)	-.001 (1,1,1)	-.08 (1,1,1)	+.02 (1,1,2)	.58
	2	-.05 (0,0,1)	-.023 (1,1,1)	-.18 (0,0,1)	+.07 (1,1,1)	.44
	3	+.04 (0,0,0)	-.005 (1,1,1)	-.02 (0,0,0)	+.01 (1,1,1)	.45
	4-5	-.002 (1,1,1)	+.002 (1,1,1)	-.05 (1,1,1)	+.0004 (1,1,1)	.69
2-1-2b	1	+.27 (3,3,3)	-.09 (3,3,3)	-.03 (0,0,1)	+.01 (2,2,3)	.58
	2	-.05 (1,1,1)	-.003 (1,1,1)	-.22 (1,1,1)	-.03 (1,1,1)	.40
	3	-.13 (2,2,3)	+.03 (3,3,3)	-.28 (3,3,3)	+.02 (2,2,3)	.77
	4	-.01 (0,1,1)	+.007 (0,1,1)	-.13 (0,0,0)	+.01 (0,0,1)	.69
	5	+.02 (1,1,1)	-.001 (0,0,0)	-.15 (0,0,0)	+.06 (1,1,1)	.67

Table H3 (Continued)

Model	Region	a_1	a_2	a_3	a_4	R^2
2-3-2a	1	+.04 (0,1,2)	+.0001(0,0,0)	+ .10 (3,3,3)		.65
	2	+.05 (3,4,4)	+.0002(0,0,0)	+ .02 (3,3,4)		.49
	3	+.05 (2,2,2)	+.0001(0,0,0)	+ .01 (1,1,2)		.47
	4-5	+.05 (3,3,3)	+.0002(1,1,2)	+ .02 (2,3,4)		.69
2-3-2b	1	+.25 (2,3,3)	-.0063(1,2,3)	- .002(0,0,1)		.48
	2	-.13 (1,1,1)	-.0008(1,1,1)	+ .009(1,1,1)		.49
	3	+.04 (2,2,2)	+.0006(0,0,1)	+ .011(1,1,1)		.68
	4	+.05 (2,2,2)	+.0005(0,0,1)	+ .014(2,2,2)		.58
	5	+.07 (2,2,2)	-.0002(0,1,1)	+ .016(1,1,1)		.63

[a]Model structures and subscript explanations are presented in the notes to Table H2.

[b]Regional divisions are discussed in Appendix G and are portrayed in Figure G1. Region 1 contained three companies, region 2 had five, region 3 had four, region 4 had four after 1896, region 5 had three after 1896, and combined regions 4 and 5 had five companies before 1896.

[c]The R^2 listed is the mean of the squared coefficients of multiple correlation of the company time series in the specified region corrected for the number of degrees of freedom.

BIBLIOGRAPHY

A. Public Documents

State

California. Commission of Transportation. Annual Report,
1877-1878.

_____. Board of Railroad Commissioners. "Annual Report,"
in California Journals of State and Assembly, 1882- .

Connecticut. Railroad Commissioners. "Annual Report," in
Connecticut Public Documents, 1877- .

Dakota. Railroad Commission. Annual Report, 1884-1889.

Illinois. Railroad and Warehouse Commission. Annual
Report, 1872-1913.

Iowa. Railroad Commission. "Railroad Commissioners Report,"
in Iowa Documents, 1898- .

Kansas. Board of Railroad Commissioners. Annual Report,
1883-1897.

Massachusetts. Railroad Commission. "Railroad Commissioners
Report," in Massachusetts Public Documents, 1870- .

Minnesota. Railroad and Warehouse Commission. Annual
Report, 1909-1936.

New York. Engineer and Surveyor. Annual Report, 1851-1922.

_____. Engineer and Surveyor. Annual Report of the
State Engineer and Surveyor in Relation to Railroad
Reports, 1849-1871.

_____. Railroad Commissioner. Annual Report, 1896-1906.

Ohio. Board of Public Works. Annual Report, 1837-1905.

_____. Department of Internal Affairs. Annual Report.
Part IV. Railroad, Canal, Telegraph and Telephone
Companies, 1875-1900.

Pennsylvania. Secretary of Internal Affairs. Annual Report,
Part III, Industrial Statistics, 1875-1913.

Virginia. Board of Public Works. Annual Report, 1860-1877.

Wisconsin. Railroad Commission. Annual Report, 1905-1931.

Federal

United States Bureau of the Census. Compendium of the Ninth Census. Washington, D.C.: 1872.

_____. Ninth Census of the United States, 1870, Vol. III, Statistics of Wealth and Industry. Washington, D.C.: 1872.

_____. Compendium of the Tenth Census. Washington, D.C.: 1883.

_____. Tenth Census of the United States, 1880, Vol. IV, Transportation. Washington, D.C.: 1880.

_____. Eleventh Census of the United States, 1890, Vol. XIV, Transportation. Washington, D.C.: 1895.

_____. Thirteenth Census of the United States, 1910, Vol. V, General Report and Analysis. Washington, D.C.: 1913.

_____. Historical Statistics of the United States. Washington, D.C.: 1960.

_____. Long Term Economic Growth 1860-1965. Washington, D.C.: 1966.

United States Commissioner of Railroads. Annual Report. Washington, D.C.: 1877-1900.

United States Congress, Joint Economic Committee. Measures of Productive Capacity. 87th Cong., May, 1962.

United States Interstate Commerce Commission. Annual Report. Washington, D.C.: 1887-1915.

_____. Statistics of Railways in the United States, Washington, D.C.: 1888- .

United States Senate. Wholesale Prices, Wages, and Transportation. Report No. 1394, 52nd Cong., 2nd Session. 1893.

B. Secondary Sources

Articles

Abbott, Edith. "The Wages of Unskilled Labor in the United States, 1850-1900," Journal of Political Economy (1905), pp. 321-367.

Abramowitz, Moses. "Resource and Output Trends in the United States Since 1870," American Economic Review (May, 1956) pp. 5-23.

Anderson, Paul S. "The Apparent Decline in Capital-Output Ratio," Quarterly Journal of Economics (November,1961), pp. 615-634.

Arrow, Kenneth J. "Alternative Approaches to the Theory of Choice in Risk-Taking Situations," Econometrica (October, 1951), pp. 404-437.

Ashton, Herbert. "Railroad Costs and Volume of Traffic," American Economic Review (June, 1940), pp. 324-332.

Barna, Tibor. "On Measuring Capital," in The Theory of Capital. Lutz, Friedrich A. ed. London: MacMillan and Co., 1963, pp. 75-94.

Borts, George H. "Production Relations in the Railway Industry," Econometrica (January, 1952), pp. 71-79.

Broster, E. J. "Variability of Railway Operating Costs," Economic Journal (1938), pp. 674-684.

Brady, Dorothy. "Relative Prices in the Nineteenth Century," Journal of Economic History (June, 1944), pp. 145-203.

_____. "Price Deflators for Final Product Estimates," in Output, Employment, and Productivity in the United States after 1800. NBER, Studies in Income and Wealth, Vol. 30. New York: Columbia University Press, 1965, pp. 91-116.

Brown, Murray. "A Measure of Technological Change and Returns to Scale," The Review of Economics and Statistics (November, 1962), pp. 402-411.

Carson, Daniel. "Changes in the Industrial Composition of Manpower since the Civil War," in Studies in Income and Wealth, Vol. 11. New York: NBER, 1949, pp. 50-133.

Chenery, Hollis. "Overcapacity and the Acceleration Principle," Econometrica (January, 1952), pp. 1-28.

Clark, John M. "Business Acceleration and the Law of Demand; A Technical Factor in Business Cycles," Journal of Political Economy (March, 1917), pp. 217-235.

Cootner, Paul H. "The Role of the Railroads in United States Economic Growth," Journal of Economic History (December, 1963), pp. 477-521.

David, Paul A. "Transport Innovation and Economic Growth," Economic History Review (December, 1969), pp. 506-525.

deLeeuw, Frank. "A Revised Index of Manufacturing Capacity," Federal Reserve Bulletin (November, 1966), pp. 1604-1615.

Eisner, Robert. "A Distributed Lag Investment Function," Econometrica (January, 1960), pp. 1-29.

_____ and Strotz, R. "The Determinants of Business Investment," Impacts of Monetary Policy. Commission on Money and Credit Research Monograph. Englewood Cliffs, New Jersey: Prentice-Hall, 1963.

_____. "Investment and the Frustrations of Econometricians," American Economic Review (March, 1969), pp. 50-64.

Fels, Rendigs. "American Business Cycles 1865-1879," American Economic Review (June, 1951), pp. 325-349.

_____. "The American Business Cycle of 1879-1885," Journal of Political Economy (February, 1952), pp. 60-75.

Fishlow, Albert. "Productivity and Technological Change in the Railroad Sector, 1840-1910," Output, Employment, and Productivity in the United States after 1800. NBER, Studies in Income and Wealth, Vol. 30. New York: Columbia University Press, 1965, pp. 583-646.

Fogel, Robert. "A Quantitative Approach to the Study of Railroads in American Economic Growth," Journal of Economic History (June, 1962), pp. 163-197.

_____. "Railroads as an Analogy to the Space Effort: Some Economic Aspects," Economic Journal (March, 1966), pp. 16-43.

Griliches, Zvi. "Capital Stock in Investment Functions: Some Problems of Concept and Measurement," Measurement in Economics. Christ, Carl F. et. al. Stanford: Stanford University Press, 1963, pp. 115-137.

_____. "Hedonic Price Indices for Automobiles," in The Price Statistics of the Federal Government. General Series No. 73. Princeton: Princeton University Press for NBER, 1961, pp. 173-196.

_____, and Jorgenson, Dale. "Sources of Measured Productivity Change: Capital Input," American Economic Review (May, 1966), pp. 50-61.

_____, and Grunfeld, Yehuda. "Is Aggregation Necessarily Bad?" Review of Economics and Statistics (January, 1960), pp. 1-13.

Grunfeld, Yehuda. "The Determinants of Corporate Investment," The Demand for Durable Goods. Arnold C. Harberger ed. Chicago: University of Chicago Press, 1960, pp. 211-266.

_____. "Interpretation of Cross-Section Estimates in a Dynamic Model," Econometrica (July, 1961), pp. 397-404.

Healey, Kent T. "Transportation as a Factor in Economic Growth," Journal of Economic History (December, 1947), pp. 87-98.

_____. "Development of a National System of Transportation," in Growth of the American Economy, Williamson, Harold F. ed. (New York: Prentice Hall, 1944), pp. 521-551.

Hurwicz, Leonid. "Least Squares Bias in Time Series," in Statistical Inference in Dynamic Economic Models. Koopmans, Tjalling C. (ed.). New York: Cowles Commission, 1950, pp. 365-384.

Jenks, Leland Hamilton. "Railroads as an Economic Force in American Development," Journal of Economic History (1944), pp. 1-20.

Jorgenson, Dale W. "Capital Theory and Investment Behavior," American Economic Review (May, 1963), pp. 247-259.

_____. "Rational Distributed Lag Functions," Econometrica (January, 1966), pp. 135-148.

_____, and Griliches, Zvi. "The Explanation of Productivity Change," The Review of Economic Studies (July, 1967), pp. 249-284.

292

Klein, Lawrence R. "Studies in Investment Behavior: Railroad Investment in the United States," in Conference on Business Cycles. New York: NBER, 1951, pp. 233-303.

Kmenta, Jan and Williamson, Jeffrey. "Determinants of Investment Behavior: United States Railroads 1872-1941," The Review of Economics and Statistics (May, 1966), pp. 172-181.

Kuh, Edwin. "The Validity of Cross-Sectionally Estimated Behavior Equations in Time Series Applications," Econometrica (April, 1959), pp. 197-214.

_____. "Theory and Institutions in the Study of Investment Behavior," American Economic Review (May, 1963), pp. 260-268.

_____, and Meyer, John R. "Investment, Liquidity, and Monetary Policy," Impacts of Monetary Policy, Commission on Money and Credit Monograph. Englewood Cliffs, New Jersey: Prentice-Hall, 1963.

Kuznets, Simon. "Relation Between Capital Goods and Finished Products in the Business Cycle," in Economic Essays in Honour of Wesley Clair Mitchell. New York: 1935.

Lebergott, Stanley. "Labor Force and Employment, 1860-1960." Output, Employment, and Productivity in the United States After 1800. NBER, Studies in Income and Wealth, Vol. 30, New York: Columbia University Press, 1965, pp. 117-204.

_____. "United States Transport Advance and Externalities," Journal of Economic History (December, 1966), pp. 437-461.

Leontieff, Wassily. "A Comment on Klein's Studies in Investment Behavior," Conference on Business Cycles. New York: NBER, 1951, pp. 310-312.

Lintner, John. "Dividends, Earnings, Leverage, Stock Prices, and the Supply of Capital to Corporations," Review of Economics and Statistics (August, 1962), pp. 243-269.

Manne, Alan S. "Some Notes on the Acceleration Principle," Review of Economics and Statistics (May, 1945), pp. 93-99.

Massell, B. F. "Capital Formation and Technological Change in United States Manufacturing," The Review of Economics and Statistics (May, 1960), pp. 182-188.

McClelland, Peter. "Railroads, American Growth, and the New Economic History: A Critique," Journal of Economic History (March, 1968), pp. 102-123.

Mitchell, Wesley C. "The Prices of American Stocks, 1890-1909," Journal of Political Economy (May, 1910), pp. 345-380.

Modigliani, Franco and Miller, Merton H. "The Cost of Capital, Corporation Finance and the Theory of Investment," American Economic Review (June, 1958), pp. 261-297.

Neal, Larry. "Investment Behavior by American Railroads: 1897-1914," Review of Economics and Statistics (May, 1969), pp. 126-135.

Nerlove, Marc. "Railroads and American Economic Growth," Journal of Economic History (March, 1966), pp. 107-115.

Noyes, Alexander D. "The Recent Economic History of the United States," Quarterly Journal of Economics (February, 1896), pp. 167-209.

Richter, Marcel K. "Invariance Axioms and Economic Indexes," Econometrica (October, 1966), pp. 739-755.

Samuelson, Paul. "Parable and Realism in Capital Theory: The Surrogate Production Function," The Review of Economic Studies (June, 1962), pp. 193-206.

Solow, Robert. "Technical Change and the Aggregate Production Function," The Review of Economics and Statistics (August, 1957), pp. 312-320.

_____. "The Production Function and the Theory of Capital," The Review of Economic Studies (June, 1956) pp. 101-108.

_____. "Technical Progress, Capital Formation and Economic Growth," American Economic Review (May, 1962), pp. 76-86.

Tinbergen, Jan. "Statistical Evidence on the Acceleration Principle," Economica (May, 1938), pp. 164-176.

VanAuken, A. M. "Preliminary Investigation of New Railway Projects," Railway Age Gazette (March 8, 1912), pp. 427-429.

Walters, A. A. "Production and Cost Functions: An Econometric Survey," Econometrica (January-April, 1963), pp. 1-66.

Williams, E. W. "Railroad Traffic Costs," American Economic Review (1943), pp. 360-365.

Books

Adams, Henry C. American Railway Accounting. New York: Henry Holt and Co., 1918.

Alexander, Edwin P. American Locomotives. New York: W. W. Norton and Co., Inc., 1950.

_____. The Pennsylvania Railroad. New York: W. W. Norton and Co., Inc., 1947.

American Locomotive Company. Exhibit at the Louisiana Purchase Exposition. New York: American Locomotive Co., 1904.

Barger, Harold. The Transportation Industries 1889-1946: A Study of Output, Employment, and Productivity. New York: NBER, 1951.

Barnaby, H. C. Analysis of Railroad Reports. New York: Metropolitan Advertising Co., 1902.

Beebe, Lucius. Mansions on Rails. Berkeley: Howell-North, 1959.

Brown, A. J. Youngson. The American Economy 1860-1940. New York: Library Publishers, 1951.

Brown, Murray. On the Theory and Measurement of Technological Change. Cambridge: Cambridge University Press, 1966.

Burgess, George H. and Kennedy, Miles C. Centennial History of the Pennsylvania Railroad Company. Philadelphia: Pennsylvania Railroad Company, 1949.

Campbell, E. G. The Reorganization of the American Railroad System, 1893-1900. New York: Columbia University Press, 1938.

Christ, Carl F. Econometric Models and Methods. New York: John Wiley and Sons, Inc. 1966.

_____, et. al. Measurement in Economics. Stanford: Stanford University Press, 1963.

Cleveland, Frederick A. and Powell, Fred W. Railroad Finance. New York: Appleton Co., 1912.

_____. Railroad Promotion and Capitalization in the United States. New York: Longmans, Green Co., 1909.

Conference in Income and Wealth. Trends in the American Economy in the Nineteenth Century, Studies in Income and Wealth, Vol. 24. Princeton: Princeton University Press for NBER, 1960.

_____. Output, Employment, and Productivity in the United States after 1800, Studies in Income and Wealth, Vol. 30. New York: Columbia University Press for NBER, 1965.

_____. Problems of Capital Formation: Concepts, Measurement and Controlling Factors, Studies in Income and Wealth, Vol. 19. Princeton: Princeton University Press for NBER, 1957.

Corbin, Bernard and Kerka, William. Steam Locomotives of the Burlington Route. Red Oak, Iowa: Thomas Murphy, Co., 1960.

Corliss, Carlton J. Mainline of Mid-America: The Story of the Illinois Central. New York: Creative Age Press, 1950.

Crandall, Bruce V. Track Labor Cost Data. Chicago: By the author, 1920.

Denison, Edward. The Sources of Economic Growth in the United States and the Alternatives Before Us. New York: Committee for Economic Development, 1962.

Derrick, Samuel M. Centennial History of the South Carolina Railroad. Columbia, South Carolina: The State Co., 1930.

Duesenberry, James S. Business Cycles and Economic Growth. New York: McGraw-Hill Book Co., 1958.

Ellis, Hamilton. Nineteenth Century Railway Carriages. London: Modern Transport Publishing Co., Ltd., 1949.

Fair, Marvin L. and Williams, Ernest W. Economics of Transportation. New York: Harper and Bros., 1950.

Faulkner, Harold U. American Economic History. 8th ed. revised. New York: Harper and Row, 1966.

_____. The Decline of Laissez Faire 1897-1917, Vol. VII of The Economic History of the United States. New York: Rinehart and Co., 1951.

Fels, Rendigs. American Business Cycles, 1865-1897. Chapel Hill: University of North Carolina Press, 1959.

Fishlow, Albert. American Railroads and the Transformation of the Ante-Bellum Economy. Cambridge: Harvard University Press, 1965.

Fogel, Robert W. Railroads and American Economic Growth: Essays in Econometric History. Baltimore: Johns Hopkins Press, 1964.

_____. The Union Pacific Railroad: A Case in Premature Enterprise. Baltimore: The Johns Hopkins Press, 1960.

Forney, M. N. Locomotives and Locomotive Building. New York: 1886.

Fromm, Gary (ed.). Transport Investment and Economic Development. Washington, D. C.: The Brookings Institution, 1965.

Fowler, George L. (ed.) Forney's Catechism of the Locomotive, Part I. 3rd ed. revised. New York: The Railway Age Gazette.

Gates, Paul W. The Illinois Central and Its Colonization Work. Cambridge: Harvard University Press, 1934.

Goldberger, Arthur S. Econometric Theory. New York: John Wiley and Sons, Inc., 1964.

Goodrich, Carter. Government Promotion of American Canals and Railroads. New York: Columbia University Press, 1961.

Green, H. A. John. Aggregation in Economic Analysis. Princeton: Princeton University Press, 1964.

Haavelmo, Trygve. A Study in the Theory of Investment. Chicago: Chicago University Press, 1961.

Habakkuk, H. J. American and British Technology in the Nineteenth Century. Cambridge: Cambridge University Press, 1962.

Hadley, Arthur T. Railroad Transportation, Its History and Laws. New York: G. P. Putnam's Sons, 1899.

Herb, Kincaid A. The Louisville and Nashville Railroad. 2nd ed. revised. Louisville: Louisville and Nashville Public Relations Dept., 1964.

Hitt, Rodney (ed.) The Car Builder's Dictionary. New York: The Railroad Gazette, 1906.

Johnson, Emery R. Principles of Railroad Transportation. New York: Appleton and Co., 1920.

Johnston, J. Econometric Methods. New York: McGraw-Hill Book Co., Inc., 1963.

Josephson, Matthew. The Robber Barrons. New York: Harcourt, Brace, and Co., 1934.

Kane, Edward J. Economic Statistics and Econometrics. New York: Harper and Row, 1968.

Kendrick, John. Productivity Trends in the United States. Princeton. Princeton University Press for NBER, 1961.

Klein, Lawrence R. Textbook of Econometrics. New York: Row, Peterson and Co., 1953.

Kolko, Gabriel. Railroads and Regulation 1877-1916. Princeton: Princeton University Press, 1965.

Koyck, L. M. Distributed Lags and Investment Analysis. Amsterdam: North Holland Publishing Co., 1954.

Kuh, Edwin. Capital Stock Growth: A Micro-Econometric Approach. Amsterdam: North Holland Publishing Co., 1963.

Kuznets, Simon. Capital in the American Economy. Princeton: Princeton University Press, 1961.

Lave, Lester. Technological Change: Its Conception and Measurement. Englewood Cliffs, New Jersey: Prentice Hall, 1966.

Locklin, D. Philip. Economics of Transportation. 5th ed. revised. Homewood, Illinois: D. Irwin, Inc., 1960.

Long, Clarence D. Wages and Earnings in the United States 1860-1890. Princeton: Princeton University Press for NBER, 1960.

Lutz, Friedrich A. and Lutz, Vera C. The Theory of Invest-
     ment of the Firm. Princeton: Princeton University
     Press, 1951.

_____ (ed.) The Theory of Capital. London: MacMillan and
     Co., 1963.

Malinvaud, E. Statistical Methods of Econometrics. 2nd ed.
     revised. New York: American Elsevier Publishing Co.,
     1970.

Mencken, August. The Railroad Passenger Car. Baltimore:
     Johns Hopkins Press, 1957.

Meyer, John R. et. al. The Economics of Competition in the
     Transportation Industries. Cambridge: Harvard Univer-
     sity Press, 1959.

_____, and Kuh, Edwin. The Investment Decision. 3rd ed.
     Cambridge: Harvard University Press, 1966.

_____, and Glauber, Robert R. Investment Decisions,
     Economic Forecasting, and Public Policy. Boston:
     Graduate School of Business Administration, Harvard
     University, 1964.

Nelson, James C. Railroad Transportation and Public Policy.
     Washington, D. C.: Brookings Institute, 1959.

Nelson, Ralph L. Merger Movements in American Industry
     1895-1956. Princeton: Princeton University Press, 1959.

Overton, Richard C. Burlington West. Cambridge: Harvard
     University Press, 1941.

Pegrum, Dudley F. Transportation: Economics and Public
     Policy. Homewood, Illinois: Irwin, 1963.

Perry, H. M. Repairs of Railway Car Equipment. Chicago:
     The Railway Age, 1899.

Pratt, Edwin. American Railways. London: MacMillan and Co.,
     1903.

Riegel, Robert Edgar. The Story of the Western Railroads.
     New York: MacMillan and Co., 1926.

Ringwalt, John L. Development of Transportation Systems in
     the United States. Philadelphia: 1888.

Ripley, William Z. Railroads, Finance and Organization. New
     York: Longmans, Green, and Co., 1915.

_____. Railroads: Rates and Regulation. New York: Longmans, Green, and Co., 1912.

Robertson, Ross M. History of the American Economy. New York: Harcourt, Brace and World, Inc., 1964.

Roper, Stephen. Handbook of the Locomotive. 14th ed. revised. Philadelphia: Edward Mecks, 1889.

Sakolski, A. M. American Railroad Economics. New York: The MacMillan Co., 1913.

Salter, W. E. G. Productivity and Technical Change. Cambridge: Cambridge University Press, 1960.

Schmookler, Jacob. Invention and Economic Growth. Cambridge: Harvard University Press, 1966.

Schumpeter, Joseph A. Business Cycles. 2 Vols. New York: McGraw Hill, 1939.

Shaw, William H. Value of Commodity Output Since 1869. New York: NBER, 1947.

Snyder, Carl. Business Cycles and Business Measurements. New York: The MacMillan Co., 1927.

Solow, Robert M. Capital Theory and the Rate of Return. Chicago: Rand McNally and Co., 1964.

Stover, John F. American Railroads. Chicago: University of Chicago Press, 1961.

_____. The Railroads of the South, 1865-1900. Chapel Hill: University of North Carolina Press, 1955.

Taylor, George R. and Neu, Irene. The American Railroad Network, 1861-1890. Cambridge: Harvard University Press, 1956.

Temin, Peter. Iron and Steel in Nineteenth-Century America. Cambridge: Massachusetts Institute of Technology Press, 1964.

Thiel, Henry. Linear Aggregation of Economic Relations. Amsterdam: North Holland Publishing Co., 1954.

Tinbergen, Jan. Statistical Testing of Business Cycle Theories. Geneva: League of Nations, 1938.

Ulmer, Melville. Capital in Transportation, Communications

and Public Utilities: Its Formation and Financing. Princeton: Princeton University Press for NBER, 1960.

_____. Trends and Cycles in Capital Formation by United States Railroads, 1870-1950. Occasional Paper 43. New York: NBER, 1954.

Warner, Paul T. Locomotives of the Pennsylvania Railroad 1834-1924. Chicago: Owen Davies, 1959.

Warren, George F. and Pearson, Frank A. Gold and Prices. New York: John Wiley and Sons, Inc., 1935.

Wellington, A. M. The Economic Theory of the Location of the Railways. 6th ed. corrected. New York: John Wiley and Sons, 1906.

White, John H., Jr. American Locomotives: An Engineering History: 1830-1880. Baltimore: Johns Hopkins Press, 1968.

Williamson, Harold F. (ed.) The Growth of the American Economy. New York: Prentice Hall, 1951.

Wilson, William H. History of the Pennsylvania Railroad. 2 Vols. Philadelphia: 1899.

Woodlock, Thomas F. The Anatomy of a Railroad Report. United States Book Co., 1895.

Zellner, Arnold (ed.). Readings in Economic Statistics and Econometrics. Boston: Little, Brown and Co., 1968.

C. Serials

American Iron and Steel Association. Annual Statistical Report. Philadelphia: 1872-

American Railroad Association. Proceedings. New York: 1886- . Annual.

American Railroad Journal. New York: 1832-1911. Weekly.

(The) Official Railway Equipment Register. New York: 1902- . Annual.

Poor's Manual of the Railroads of the United States. New York: 1868- . Annual.

Railroad (Age) Gazette. New York: 1873-   Weekly.

Railway and Locomotive Historical Society. Bulletin.
    Boston: 1922-

Railway Monitor. New York: 1873-1874. Weekly.

Railway World. New York: 1875-1915. Weekly.

Dissertations in American Economic History

An Arno Press Collection

Adams, Donald R., Jr. **Wage Rates in Philadelphia, 1790-1830.**
(Doctoral Dissertation, University of Pennsylvania, 1967). 1975

Aldrich, Terry Mark. **Rates of Return on Investment in Technical
Education in the Ante-Bellum American Economy.** (Doctoral
Dissertation, The University of Texas at Austin, 1969). 1975

Anderson, Terry Lee. **The Economic Growth of Seventeenth
Century New England:** A Measurement of Regional Income.
(Doctoral Dissertation, University of Washington, 1972). 1975

Bean, Richard Nelson. **The British Trans-Atlantic Slave Trade,
1650-1775.** (Doctoral Dissertation, University of Washington,
1971). 1975

Brock, Leslie V. **The Currency of the American Colonies,
1700-1764:** A Study in Colonial Finance and Imperial Relations.
(Doctoral Dissertation, University of Michigan, 1941). 1975

Ellsworth, Lucius F. **Craft to National Industry in the Nineteenth
Century:** A Case Study of the Transformation of the New York
State Tanning Industry. (Doctoral Dissertation, University of
Delaware, 1971). 1975

Fleisig, Heywood W. **Long Term Capital Flows and the Great
Depression:** The Role of the United States, 1927-1933.
(Doctoral Dissertation, Yale University, 1969). 1975

Foust, James D. **The Yeoman Farmer and Westward Expansion
of U. S. Cotton Production.** (Doctoral Dissertation, University of
North Carolina at Chapel Hill, 1968). 1975

Golden, James Reed. **Investment Behavior By United States
Railroads, 1870-1914.** (Doctoral Thesis, Harvard University,
1971). 1975

Hill, Peter Jensen. **The Economic Impact of Immigration into the
United States.** (Doctoral Dissertation, The University of Chicago,
1970). 1975

Klingaman, David C. **Colonial Virginia's Coastwise and Grain
Trade.** (Doctoral Dissertation, University of Virginia, 1967). 1975

Lang, Edith Mae. **The Effects of Net Interregional Migration on
Agricultural Income Growth:** The United States, 1850-1860.
(Doctoral Thesis, The University of Rochester, 1971). 1975

Lindley, Lester G. **The Constitution Faces Technology:**
The Relationship of the National Government to the Telegraph,
1866-1884. (Doctoral Thesis, Rice University, 1971). 1975

Lorant, John H[erman]. **The Role of Capital-Improving
Innovations in American Manufacturing During the 1920's.**
(Doctoral Thesis, Columbia University, 1966). 1975

Mishkin, David Joel. **The American Colonial Wine Industry:** An Economic Interpretation, Volumes I and II. (Doctoral Thesis, University of Illinois, 1966). 1975

Oates, Mary J. **The Role of the Cotton Textile Industry in the Economic Development of the American Southeast:** 1900-1940. (Doctoral Dissertation, Yale University, 1969). 1975

Passell, Peter. **Essays in the Economics of Nineteenth Century American Land Policy.** (Doctoral Dissertation, Yale University, 1970). 1975

Pope, Clayne L. **The Impact of the Ante-Bellum Tariff on Income Distribution.** (Doctoral Dissertation, The University of Chicago, 1972). 1975

Poulson, Barry Warren. **Value Added in Manufacturing, Mining, and Agriculture in the American Economy From 1809 To 1839.** (Doctoral Dissertation, The Ohio State University, 1965). 1975

Rockoff, Hugh. **The Free Banking Era: A Re-Examination.** (Doctoral Dissertation, The University of Chicago, 1972). 1975

Schumacher, Max George. **The Northern Farmer and His Markets During the Late Colonial Period.** (Doctoral Dissertation, University of California at Berkeley, 1948). 1975

Seagrave, Charles Edwin. **The Southern Negro Agricultural Worker:** 1850-1870. (Doctoral Dissertation, Stanford University, 1971). 1975

Solmon, Lewis C. **Capital Formation by Expenditures on Formal Education, 1880 and 1890.** (Doctoral Dissertation, The University of Chicago, 1968). 1975

Swan, Dale Evans. **The Structure and Profitability of the Antebellum Rice Industry:** 1859. (Doctoral Dissertation, University of North Carolina at Chapel Hill, 1972). 1975

Sylla, Richard Eugene. **The American Capital Market, 1846-1914:** A Study of the Effects of Public Policy on Economic Development. (Doctoral Thesis, Harvard University, 1968) 1975

Uselding, Paul John. **Studies in the Technological Development of the American Economy During the First Half of the Nineteenth Century.** (Doctoral Dissertation, Northwestern University, 1970) 1975

Walsh, William D[avid]. **The Diffusion of Technological Change in the Pennsylvania Pig Iron Industry, 1850-1870.** (Doctoral Dissertation, Yale University, 1967). 1975

Weiss, Thomas Joseph. **The Service Sector in the United States, 1839 Through 1899.** (Doctoral Thesis, University of North Carolina at Chapel Hill, 1967). 1975

Zevin, Robert Brooke. **The Growth of Manufacturing in Early Nineteenth Century New England.** 1975